To the memory of my father,
Richard Jarvis Brown

He always loved the Adirondacks.

Fall Stream Photo by Mark Bowie

ADIRONDACK PADDLING

60 Great Flatwater Adventures

BY PHIL BROWN

LOST POND PRESS

Saranac Lake, NY

2012

Adirondack
ADK
Mountain Club

Published by Lost Pond Press and the Adirondack Mountain Club.

Lost Pond Press
50 Cliff Road, Unit 4, Saranac Lake, NY 12983
www.lostpondpress.com

Adirondack Mountain Club
814 Goggins Road, Lake George, NY 12845-4117
518-668-4447 www.adk.org

Design by Susan Bibeau
Beehive Productions, Saranac Lake, NY

Maps by Matt Paul

Cover photo by Susan Bibeau
North Branch of the Saranac River

Back cover photo by Phil Brown
Oseetah Lake

ISBN: 978-0-9789254-1-3

Library of Congress Control Number: 2012911018

Printed by Versa Press

Acknowledgements

Thanks go first to the Adirondack Mountain Club, my co-publisher. Neil Woodworth, the executive director, and his able assistants, John Million and John Kettlewell, saw a need in the Adirondacks for a full-color flatwater guidebook and had faith in my ability to produce it.

A number of people contributed their talents to the project. As she has with other Lost Pond Press books, Susan Bibeau did a superb job with the design. Matt Paul once again demonstrated his skill as a mapmaker.

Larry Master generously donated many images of flowers and wildlife. Several other professional photographers allowed me to use their images, greatly enhancing the book's visual appeal. Thanks to Carl Heilman II, Mark Bowie, Nancy Ford, Susan Bibeau, Ray Palmer, Don Cochran, and others who gave me photos.

I want to single out Mike Lynch for special mention. Although I paddled all the routes in this book, I couldn't get back to some to check mileages and other facts. Mike did these routes and shared his notes with me. He also let me use some of his photos and gave a first read to many of the chapters.

Mary Thill caught many errors in the manuscript and made many helpful suggestions, proving the value of good copy-editing. My friend Mike Virtanen and colleague Betsy Dirnberger also prevented a number of mistakes from seeing the light of day.

A tip of the Sombrero (my favorite paddling hat) to Outdoor Research for letting me test their clothing, dry bags, and other gear.

Finally, I want to thank everyone at the *Adirondack Explorer*, where I have worked for the past twelve years. The *Explorer*'s mission is to protect the Adirondack Park. If you paddle the waterways in this book, I think you'll agree that it's a place worth saving.

—**Phil Brown**

Introduction

Every guidebook betrays the prejudices of its author. Mine are revealed by the chapter on Alder Bed Flow, a marsh on the Middle Branch of the Oswegatchie River.

If you haven't heard of it, that's not surprising. Alder Bed Flow is rarely visited for the simple reason that it's hard to get to. I'm referring not only to the long drive over a dirt road to the unmarked put-in, but also to the shallow riffles in the first half-mile of the paddle. On most days you'll frequently be scraping bottom or walking your boat. Although Alder Bed Flow is remote and peaceful, who would go through that much trouble for a few hours in paradise?

Well, some people. I prefer paddling wild places—the winding stream or placid pond—to large lakes abuzz with powerboats. If you too like the wild, this book is for you. And don't worry, not all the places are as hard to get to as Alder Bed Flow. In fact, most are easily accessible.

Personal prejudices notwithstanding, I could not ignore the bigger lakes of the Adirondack Park. Oftentimes they offer spectacular views of the mountains. And so you will find trips that include portions of the Saranac Lakes, Blue Mountain Lake, Rainbow Lake, Schroon Lake, Lake George, and Lake Champlain.

In short, *Adirondack Paddling: 60 Great Flatwater Adventures* reflects the park's wonderful variety of waterways, from the tiny, twisting Hatch Brook to the mighty Hudson, from the intimate charms of Bog Pond to the big-sky vistas of Oseetah Lake, from the obscure Alder Bed Flow to the ever-popular Lake George. But the book leans toward the wilder end of the spectrum.

The trips range in distance from the 3.5-mile circuit of Nelson Lake to the 23-mile round-trip to High Falls on the Oswegatchie. Some have arduous carries; some have no carries. Some are close to civilization; others are reached by bumpy rides on back roads. The common denominator is that all can be done in a day (although the appendix has suggestions for longer excursions). Also, all were chosen with flatwater paddlers in mind.

There is no Adirondack guidebook quite like this—one that covers the whole park and focuses on flatwater. Years ago, Barbara McMartin published a flatwater guidebook, but it was aimed primarily at young readers. The Adirondack Mountain Club's previous guidebooks—including the celebrated *Adirondack Canoe Waters: North Flow* by Paul Jamieson and Donald Morris—covered only sections of the park and lumped together whitewater and flatwater. Adirondack Paddling is not meant to replace

North Flow. No guidebook could do that. As a matter of fact, I quote Jamieson's fine prose many times in these pages. Yet whitewater paddling and flatwater paddling are different sports, despite the overlap in equipment and practitioners. Given flatwater's great popularity, it deserves a guidebook of its own.

A few words about safety

Whenever you venture into the wild for the day, whether by foot or by boat, you should be prepared to survive the night in case of emergency. This doesn't mean you need to tote a sleeping bag and tent on every outing, but you should at least bring the ten essentials. In recent years, the editors of the classic manual *Mountaineering: The Freedom of the Hills* changed the book's list of essential items to a list of essential "systems." The list follows:

Navigation
Sun protection
Insulation (extra clothing)
Illumination (headlamp or flashlight)
First-aid supplies
Fire
Repair kit and tools
Nutrition (extra food)
Hydration (extra water)
Emergency shelter

This approach allows the editors to sneak in a few extra items. Your navigation gear, for example, should include both map and compass, and you may want to bring a GPS unit as well. For sun protection, you should have both sunglasses and sunscreen. Your fire system should include a fire-starter, such as a candle, and a lighter or matches. The systems approach is flexible. For emergency shelter, you could bring something as lightweight as a plastic tube tent or large garbage bag or opt for a bivy sack and foam pad. Your choice will depend on the weather conditions and your desire for comfort.

Paddlers also must prepare for the possibility of a dunking. New York State law requires you to carry one life vest for each person in your canoe or kayak. Furthermore, the law requires you to wear a vest if you go paddling between November 1 and May 1. If you overturn in cold weather, you risk hypothermia, so you'll want to change fast into those extra clothes. Wet clothes won't do you much good, so always carry your extra duds and other essential items in a dry bag. Keep the bag tethered to the vessel.

Using this book

The book divides the Adirondack Park into quadrants, using highways as boundaries. Route 30 is the boundary between the east and west parts of the park. For the north-south boundary, we use the Boreas Road and the stretch of Route 28N that goes through Newcomb, following the latitudinal lines of these roads to both edges of the park. Though roughly equal in size, the quadrants do not share equally in the region's watery riches. The northwest quad, which encompasses much of the Park's lake belt and a number of major rivers, lays claim to twenty-one of the sixty routes. In contrast, the southeast quad has only six.

Each of the sixty trips is described in its own chapter. All of the paddling routes are depicted on color maps showing put-ins, takeouts, and carry trails. The routes are illustrated by color photos as well. At the head of every chapter is a summary of the trip, in the form of a list of basic information, to wit:

Length. The mileage of the trip, including carries, as measured by a GPS watch.

Carries. The number and total distance of portages. If there is only one carry, just the distance is given.

Shuttle. Indicates whether a shuttle is necessary. If so, the shuttle distance is given. In many cases, a bicycle can be used to get back to your car.

Motors. Indicates whether motorboats are prohibited or permitted. The Adirondack Park State Land Master Plan governs management of the 2.6 million acres of public Forest Preserve in the park, and it classifies most of the preserve as Wilderness or Wild Forest. Motors are prohibited in Wilderness as well as in the St. Regis Canoe Area, but they generally are permitted in Wild Forest (and on waterways bordering private land). Motorboats are banned on fourteen of the routes in this book (either the entire route or most of it). On most of the other routes, motorboats are legally permitted but seldom encountered. It seems that twisting streams with occasional shallows and beaver dams do not attract many powerboaters. Paddlers are most likely to see them on the large lakes.

WSR status. If a waterway belongs to the state's Wild, Scenic, and Recreational Rivers System, its classification is noted. The classification offers a rough guide to a river's character. A river designated Wild is remote from roads and free of development. Motorboats are banned on Wild rivers. A river designated Scenic is not as remote but remains largely free of development. Motorboats are sometimes allowed on Scenic rivers. Typically, rivers designated Recreational have more development. Motorboats are usually allowed on Recreational rivers. Waterways classified as Study Rivers were nominated for the system but never added, apparently for political reasons.

Meander quotient. A measure of a river's twistiness. The higher the quotient, the twistier the river. If you paddle a stream with a meander quotient of 50%, you are in effect paddling in the "wrong" direction half the time. Where I give a quotient, it applies only to the river portion of a trip. See the second appendix (page 269) for a fuller explanation and a table of meander quotients.

Put-in/Takeout. Latitude and longitude are given for the parking areas for put-ins and takeouts. The coordinates are presented in degrees and minutes (and fractional minutes). Driving directions to put-ins and takeouts are provided at the end of the chapters.

National Geographic map. The Adirondack Mountain Club has collaborated with National Geographic in developing the waterproof Trails Illustrated maps for the Adirondack Park. These five full-color maps cover the whole Park and show hiking trails, put-ins and takeouts, campgrounds, and other recreational facilities. The trip summary tells you which of the five maps to use for the route in question. See the Map Resources appendix (page 277) for more information on these and other maps of use to paddlers.

The chapter maps use the symbols shown below. In some cases, two paddling routes are depicted on the same map. Matt Paul of Saranac Lake created all the maps in this book.

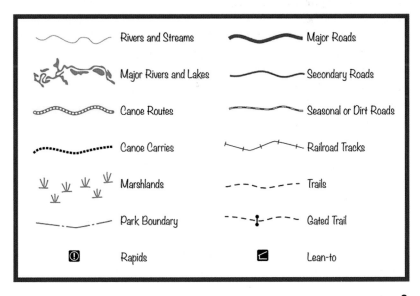

Rivers and Streams		Major Roads
Major Rivers and Lakes		Secondary Roads
Canoe Routes		Seasonal or Dirt Roads
Canoe Carries		Railroad Tracks
Marshlands		Trails
Park Boundary		Gated Trail
Rapids		Lean-to

Middle Saranac Lake. Photo by Mike Lynch

Contents

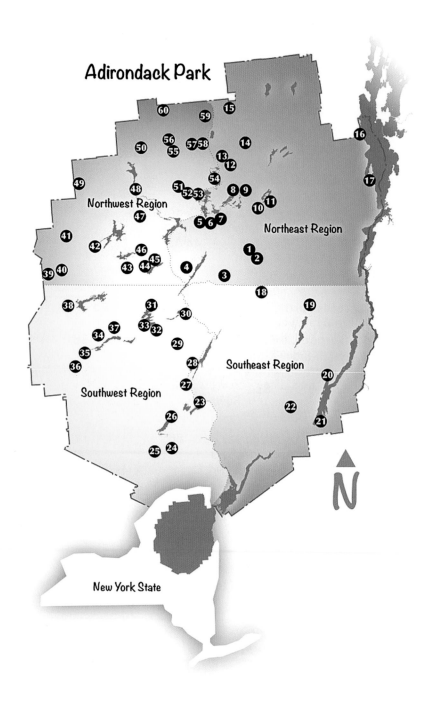

Adirondack Park

New York State

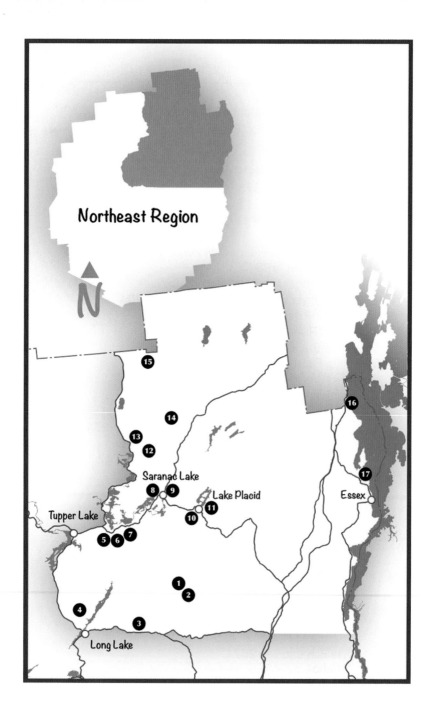

Northeast Region

N

Saranac Lake

Lake Placid

Essex

Tupper Lake

Long Lake

Saranac River meadows. Photo by Mark Bowie

NORTHEAST REGION

1. Henderson Lake to Duck Hole

Length: 12 miles round-trip

Carries: 4 totaling 2.1 miles

Shuttle: No

Motors: Prohibited

Put-in: 44°05.333' N, 74°03.376' W

National Geographic map: Lake Placid/High Peaks

The scenic Duck Hole in the remote western High Peak Wilderness had long been a favorite camping spot, and when the Open Space Institute bought Henderson Lake and the Preston Ponds in 2003, it became possible to paddle there, too (albeit with a long carry). OSI later sold the water bodies to the state.

After Tropical Storm Irene dumped ten inches of rain on the High Peaks in 2011, floodwaters breached the dam at Duck Hole, draining most of the brook-trout pond. A large pool remained on the east side of Duck Hole, and it was still possible to put in there and paddle down an outlet stream flowing through a muddy plain. And you could still take in the grand views of the mountains that encircle the pond, including a few four-thousand-footers. Over the next several years, visitors will be able to observe the transformation of the mud plain into a lush wetland.

Duck Hole was never the only reason for undertaking the long portage from Henderson Lake. Both of the Preston Ponds (Upper and Lower) are worthy destinations in their own right: wilderness lakes with stunning views of large mountains.

Those disinclined to carry the 1.7 miles to the Preston Ponds can while away a good part of a day exploring two-mile-long Henderson Lake. Like the ponds, Henderson is undeveloped and offers stupendous views—of Wallface in Indian Pass and of several High Peaks. Be sure to check out the marshes where Indian Pass Brook and Santanoni Brook enter the lake.

However far you care to venture, the journey begins with a 0.3-mile carry along abandoned gravel roads (easily wheelable) from the Upper Works parking lot to a put-in near the Henderson Lake dam, where the

Henderson Lake, looking toward Wallface. Photo by Carl Heilman II

Hudson River begins its long journey to New York City. To reach the dam, turn left onto a spur road immediately after crossing the Hudson.

Paddling up a narrow arm of the lake, you can see 4,607-foot Santanoni Peak straight ahead, but as you advance, it soon becomes obscured by Henderson Mountain, which is smaller but closer. Before leaving the arm, turn around for a view of the slide-scarred Mount Colden, another High Peak.

If you intend to go to Preston Ponds or Duck Hole, turn right upon reaching the main part of the lake and head for the little inlet on the northwest shore (listen for a waterfall as you approach). Take out to the right of the inlet and walk a short distance to a lean-to.

From the lean-to, follow a short footpath to a hiking trail and turn left. Marked by red disks, the trail is fairly level at first as it makes several stream crossings. After nearly a mile, it ascends to a small pass, then descends to a junction. The shore of Upper Preston Pond is just twenty yards to the left. Paddle down the bay and then head to Upper Preston's north end. Look for a small opening in the leatherleaf about fifty feet left of the outlet. Take out here and carry along an unmarked path less than a tenth of a mile to Lower Preston Pond.

Duck Hole after Tropical Storm Irene. Photo by Carl Heilman II

After putting in, aim for the large island on the west side of Lower Preston. You'll find the outlet on the other side of the island. Go down the shallow stream less than a quarter-mile and look for a small grassy takeout on the left, just before some rapids. (In summer, the water may be too shallow to paddle.) Do not venture down the rapids, for around the bend is a waterfall with a fifteen-foot drop. From the takeout, follow a very short path over a knoll to the pool that is now Duck Hole.

Assuming the pool remains, you should be able to put in without a problem and paddle down the outlet to the broken dam and the two Duck Hole lean-tos. You also may be able to go a quarter-mile or so up Roaring Brook, which enters the plain from the north.

Among the taller peaks that can be seen from the Preston Ponds and Duck Hole are those in the Santanoni, Sawtooth, and Seward ranges. MacNaughton Mountain is also visible for much of the trip. Perhaps someday, when overtaken by shrubs, flowers, and grasses, the muddy wasteland at Duck Hole will add its own beauty to that of the mountains.

DIRECTIONS: From Northway Exit 29, drive west on Blue Ridge Road (County 2) for 17.8 miles to the Tahawus Road (County 84). Turn right and go 6.5 to an intersection. Bear left and continue 3.6 miles to the Upper Works lot at the end of the road.

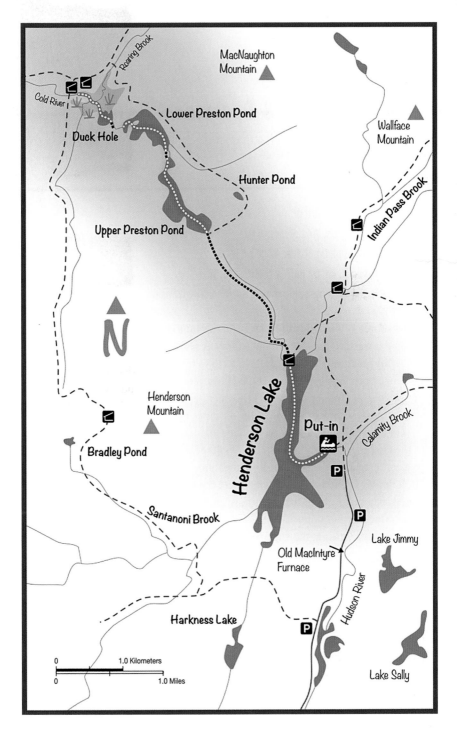

MacNaughton Mountain ▲

Roaring Brook

Cold River

Lower Preston Pond

Duck Hole

Wallface Mountain ▲

Hunter Pond

Indian Pass Brook

Upper Preston Pond

N ▲

Henderson Mountain ▲

Henderson Lake

Put-in

Calamity Brook

Bradley Pond

Santanoni Brook

Lake Jimmy

Old MacIntyre Furnace

Harkness Lake

Hudson River

Lake Sally

0   1.0 Kilometers

0   1.0 Miles

2. Upper Hudson & Opalescent Rivers

Length: 7.5 to 12.5 miles

Carries: 2 totaling 50 yards

Shuttle: 2.4 miles

Motors: Permitted

WSR status: Wild, Recreational

Put-in: 44°04.357' N, 74°03.437' W

Takeout: 44°02.606' N, 74°03.488' W

National Geographic map: Lake Placid/High Peaks

The source of the Hudson River is often said to be Lake Tear of the Clouds on the western flank of Mount Marcy. It seems fitting that a pond on the state's highest mountain should give birth to the state's mightiest river. Alas, a stronger case can be made that the Hudson begins its 315-mile journey to the Atlantic at Henderson Lake. The waters of Lake Tear reach the Hudson, via the Opalescent River, more than six miles below Henderson.

On this outing, you start on the Hudson, paddle downriver 4.5 miles to the Opalescent, then head up the Opalescent as far as three miles. The scenery is a curious mix of unspoiled nature, with stunning views of the High Peaks, and industrial blight, where the Hudson flows past an abandoned strip mine. From the takeout, it's a relaxing 2.4-mile bicycle ride back to the starting point.

As of this writing, the state was planning to buy from the Nature Conservancy a five-mile section of the Hudson below the old mine as well as the lower part of the Opalescent (the only part still in private hands). When that occurs, it should enhance public access and enjoyment of both rivers. Meantime, paddlers can put in and take out along a road that leads to the hikers' parking lot at Upper Works. The dead-end road parallels the Hudson throughout the trip. Once the state buys the river corridor, the road will provide a number of access points. Until then, legal options are limited.

One legal put-in is a few miles downriver from Henderson Lake next to an unmarked pull-off. Incidentally, a half-mile up the road is a stone blast furnace built in 1854 to smelt iron. If you haven't seen this historical curi-

Sanford Lake on the Upper Hudson River. Photo by Phil Brown

osity, it's a worth a look before you begin your trip. Also, it will set the stage for the post-industrial sights to come.

Next to the pull-off is a rock that slopes into the water. If the rock is not too slippery, you can put in here. Otherwise, walk up the road twenty yards and squeeze through the brush to the river. The Hudson is forty to fifty feet wide here, with cedars growing along the banks. It soon broadens, opening up views of the Santanoni Range in the west. Looking back, you can see a number of other large peaks as well as the magnificent cliff on Wallface. While heading downriver, keep in mind that the best views often lie behind—so turn around frequently.

About a mile from the put-in lurks a line of rocks extending across the river. You'll probably need to step out of your boat to get over the obstruction. At 1.75 miles, you reach an industrial road where the river flows through several old culverts. Take out on the left to carry over the road. The area is a moonscape of broken rock, spoils from the mine. Looking up the road, you can see an enormous mound of tailings.

Mine spoils cover the left bank for a good distance downriver. At 2.4 miles, you pass under County Route 76. You'll return here for the takeout, but for now keep going downriver. Within a half-mile, the Hudson widens into Sanford Lake. The river constricts again when it reaches a marsh. Be sure to look back here for another good view of the High Peaks. In another half-mile, the Opalescent enters from the left. The Opalescent has been designated a Wild River in the state's Wild, Scenic, and Recreational System. Because of its industrial history, the uppermost Hudson has not been part of the system to this point, but from the Opalescent to the Adirondack Park boundary it is classified as a Recreational River.

It's hard to resist the allure of a Wild River. If you're determined, you can paddle up the Opalescent at least three miles, but you likely will have to contend with shallows and an occasionally strong current. Many people will be content to go just a half-mile or mile. The river is very twisty, with sand and gravel bars on the bends. After the state buys this part of the river, paddlers will be free to beach their boats and go for a swim.

After returning to the Hudson, you can return to the takeout on Route 76 or extend the trip by continuing downriver. If you go back now, your trip will amount to 6.5 miles on the Hudson plus your miles on the Opalescent. (You could avoid a shuttle by doing a round-trip from the Route 76 bridge.) If you opt to go ahead, you could travel another five miles downriver to the County Route 25 bridge that you crossed on the way to the put-in. However, this would necessitate shooting rapids that start above the bridge. You also would have to carry around a huge logjam about three and a half miles below the Opalescent. One option is to paddle downriver about a mile, where the Hudson enters a wetland with spectacular views of Algonquin Peak, the Adirondacks' second-highest mountain. Shortly after, the river pulls close to the road, so in the future you may be able to take out here. Once the state consummates the Nature Conservancy deal, paddlers also will be able to take out at a logging-road bridge just below the mouth of Opalescent, located 4.7 miles from the put-in.

DIRECTIONS: From Northway Exit 29, drive west on the Boreas Road (also known as Blue Ridge Road) for 17.8 miles to County 25, which leads to Tahawus and the Upper Works trailhead. Turn right and go 0.6 miles to a bridge over the Hudson. This is the takeout if you want to run the rapids upstream from the bridge. If not, continue 4.9 miles to the junction with County 76. Bearing right, you immediately reach a highway bridge. This is the takeout that flatwater paddlers should use. To reach the put-in, return to County 25 and go another 2.4 miles to a small pull-off on the right next to a Forest Preserve sign. The pull-off is 0.3 miles past the turn for the Bradley Pond trail and close to the river. If you reach the old blast furnace, you've gone a half-mile too far.

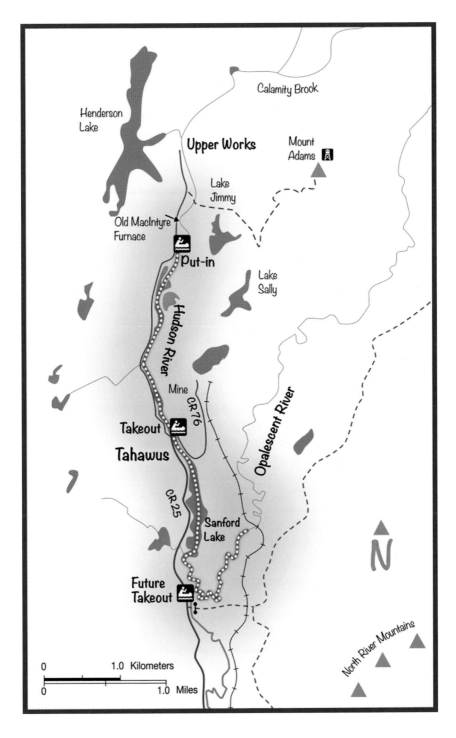

Henderson Lake

Calamity Brook

Upper Works

Mount Adams

Lake Jimmy

Old MacIntyre Furnace

Put-in

Lake Sally

Hudson River

Mine

CR 76

Opalescent River

Takeout

Tahawus

CR 25

Sanford Lake

Future Takeout

N

Sanford Lake

North River Mountains

0   1.0 Kilometers

0   1.0 Miles

3. Rich & Harris Lakes

Length: 5 to 13 miles
Carries: 2 totaling 0.2 miles
Shuttle: 4.5 miles
Motors: Permitted on Harris Lake
Put-in: 43°58.257' N, 74°11.903' W
Takeout: 43°57.958' N, 74°07.852' W
National Geographic map: Lake Placid/High Peaks

In the 1930s, Anna and Archer Huntington donated fifteen thousand acres of forestland in Newcomb to Syracuse University. Today, the New York State College of Environmental Science and Forestry uses the property to study, among other things, climate change, forest ecology, and wildlife behavior. Although most of the Huntington Wildlife Forest is off limits to the public, ESF welcomes visitors to its Adirondack Interpretive Center, which has a network of hiking and ski trails, and allows paddlers to use nearby Rich Lake, a pristine water where motors are prohibited.

Huntington Wildlife Forest is not Forest Preserve and has its own rules. Camping, fires, and hunting are prohibited. Indeed, once launched, paddlers should not land on ESF property, excepting the Interpretive Center.

From the parking lot, there is a short carry to a beach on the south shore of Rich Lake. You have a choice of two trips: paddle west across the lake to Fishing Brook and up the brook to the first rapid, a round-trip of nearly six miles, or paddle down Rich Lake's outlet to Belden Lake, Harris Lake, and finally the Hudson River, a one-way trip of five to seven miles, depending on how much of the Hudson you choose to explore.

The first trip is the wilder: you see few signs of civilization. The second offers more variety, but expect to see plenty of houses, camps, and other development. Also, motorboats are allowed on Harris Lake. If you can't make up your mind, combine the two trips for a journey of up to thirteen miles. Both are described here.

If you're heading to Fishing Brook, follow the western shore of Rich Lake to the marsh at the mouth of the stream, reached in 1.25 miles. The

The Hudson River in Newcomb. Photo by Phil Brown

marsh affords good views of the Fishing Brook Range to the southwest. In another half-mile, you pass under power lines and then a small bridge. As you head upstream, the grasses and shrubs of the marsh give way to alders and then conifer trees. You are surrounded by wildness.

Although Fishing Brook is not as winding as many Adirondack streams, it has its share of turns. At 0.65 miles from the bridge, you reach a fork. No matter which one you take, you soon encounter rapids, but going right is preferable. In a tenth of a mile, you come to a logging-road bridge, with attractive cascades on the other side. There is plenty of room to turn around in the pool near the bridge. You can poke up the other fork on the return trip.

If you plan on doing a through trip to Harris Lake and the Hudson, you need to arrange a shuttle. Cloud Splitter Outfitters in Newcomb will allow you to leave a second car at its shop, located on Route 28N next to the bridge over the river. But check with the owners first. For a fee, they will drive you back to your starting point.

From the Rich Lake put-in, paddle toward the north shore, then round a peninsula on the right and continue to the Rich Lake outlet. After rounding the peninsula, you enter a narrow arm, with views of Goodnow Mountain's fire tower to the south. Shortly you reach the outlet, passing a dock and going under a wooden footbridge on the Adirondack Interpretive Center property.

About a quarter-mile after the bridge, look for a carry trail on the left, just before a second bridge. The short trail leads around rapids to the west shore of Belden Lake. Paddle east across the small lake to a rocky outlet. If the water is low, you may have to walk your boat a little bit.

There are camps on the right below the small rapid—an indication that you have left ESF property. Continuing downstream, you encounter a few riffles and then enter a grassy marsh. At 2.7 miles from the Rich Lake put-in, you cross under the road that leads to Camp Santanoni. The channel is rocky on the other side of the bridge, so you probably will want to exit your boat.

Harris Lake starts below this short rapid. The south shore is a stone's throw from Route 28N. It has a number of homes, a boat launch, and a town beach. The north shore is Forest Preserve, undeveloped except for a state campground. In summer, especially, you are likely to see motorboats. Paddle east toward a good-size island. Soon after passing the island, bear right to follow the broad, marshy outlet to the Hudson River. Signs at the confluence point left toward Mount Marcy and right toward New York City. Head toward New York: in just a quarter-mile you reach the Route 28N bridge.

You could take out here, five miles from the original put-in, but you can extend the trip by continuing down the Hudson for a mile. You will have to contend with a short patch of quick water beneath the bridge, but the rewards are well worth this small difficulty. Below the highway, the Hudson is wide and sluggish, with marshes harboring waterfowl and with wonderful views of Vanderwhacker Mountain in the distance. Turn back when you reach rapids. On the return, you will enjoy views of the High Peaks.

DIRECTIONS: The takeout is at the NY 28N bridge over the Hudson in Newcomb. Cloud Splitter Outfitters, which is located next to the bridge, allows the public to take out on its property, but ask permission first. To reach the put-in, drive west from the bridge for 4.5 miles to Rich Lake Lane on the right. Although the road is marked private, the public is allowed to drive on the road to access the put-in. Go about 0.1 miles and turn left to reach the parking area.

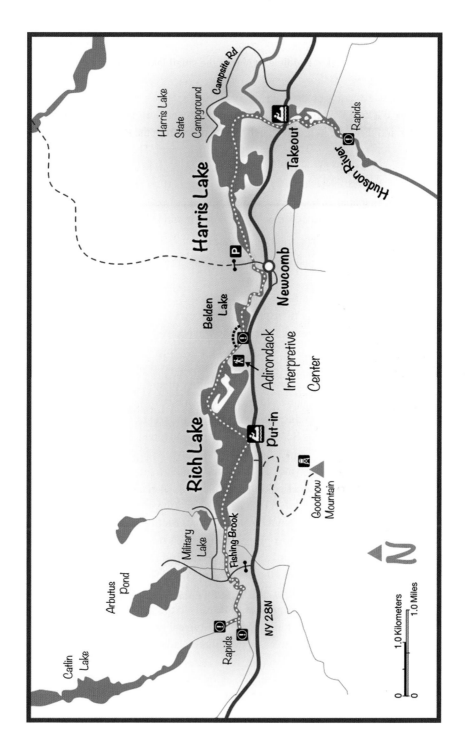

4. Cedarlands

....

Length: 6 miles round-trip

Carries: 2 totaling 0.95 miles

Shuttle: None

Motors: Prohibited

Put-in: 44°00.714' N, 74°24.942' W

National Geographic map: Lake Placid/High Peaks

You don't have to be a Boy Scout to enjoy the Cedarlands Scout Reservation, but you do have to be prepared to obey a few rules. No motorboats, no trapping, and no camping except at designated sites (as of 2012, there were none).

The centerpiece of Cedarlands is the four-hundred-acre Rock Pond, which the Scouts call McRorie Lake in memory of an Eagle Scout who died young. McRorie Lake is closed to the public in July and August, when the Scouts are there, but the public may visit it the rest of the year. The smaller Mud Pond (alias Scout Pond) is open year-round. Essentially, this means you can paddle from Mud to McRorie anytime in spring, fall, or late summer. The trip is short enough that you should have time to climb one or more of the mountains overlooking the mile-long lake.

The state intends to build a trail from the parking area to Mud Pond, but for now you reach the pond by carrying or wheeling your boat along access roads for 0.7 miles to a put-in on the pond's northeast shore. After launching, paddle west toward a large bog, with Big Brook Hills rising in the background. As you cross the pond, Mud Pond Mountain comes into view in the northwest, with Grampus Mountain peeking over its shoulder.

Approaching the bog, bear right (left leads to the outlet, which flows into Big Brook) to go up Mud's inlet. Flora typical of Adirondack bogs grow along the shores: tamarack trees, cotton grass, leatherleaf, sundews, and pitcher plants.

Heading up the broad stream, you enjoy great views across the wetland toward Rock Pond Mountain and Mud Pond Mountain. At 0.8 miles from the put-in, you reach the start of a carry trail on the right. You may have to push your way through marsh grass to find it. The trail leads around rapids

Going up the Mud Pond inlet. Photo by Susan Bibeau

to the access road. Turn left and cross the bridge over the stream. About twenty-five yards beyond the bridge, turn right to follow a short path to a put-in above the rapids. The carry from Mud Pond is about a quarter-mile.

Heading up a narrow arm of McRorie Lake, you soon reach the open water. The lake is bordered by an arc of forested peaks: Mud, Grampus, and Rock Pond mountains. (The last peak, distinguished by a wall of cliffs, is also known as Mount Masters.) Farther away, due east, is the 3,346-foot summit of Kempshall Mountain. The loftier peaks of the Seward Range lie to the northeast. Except for the Boy Scout facilities on the south shore, the lake is undeveloped. The south shore is not open to the public, but you are free to land elsewhere and take a hike, go for a swim, or have a picnic. Fishing also is allowed.

A good way to supplement the paddling adventure is to climb Mud Pond Mountain (which the Scouts call OA Mountain) for its views of McRorie Lake and the High Peaks. You could reach the trail by following the access road from the outlet bridge north for 0.85 miles, but if you're paddling, there's a better way to get there. When you first enter McRorie, straight ahead is Loon Island, the biggest island on the lake. Paddle to the left around the island (beware submerged rocks in the channel between the

Gazing down on McRorie Lake from Mud Pond Mountain. Photo by Susan Bibeau

island and the mainland) and then round a prominent point on the lake's west shore to enter a small bay. (There is a split rock in the bay that the Scouts use for swimming.) As you near the end of the bay, look on the right shore for a faint path marked by surveyor's tape (and perhaps a traffic cone).

Follow this path a hundred feet to an old woods road. Turn right and go another hundred feet to the access road. Turn left and go a hundred feet more to the trailhead on the right, marked by a sign. Follow the trail a half-mile to the Mud Pond lookout, which offers stunning views over McRorie Lake toward the High Peaks.

For a longer outing, you could also hike the Skyline Trail, which starts near the Mud Pond Mountain summit and goes over Grampus Mountain and Rock Pond Mountain. The latter also offers a splendid view over McRorie Lake. The trail eventually takes you back to the access road at the north end of the lake. You return by walking along the road back to your boat. As of 2011, the Skyline Trail was poorly marked, so until it is improved, it cannot be recommended.

DIRECTIONS: From the hamlet of Long Lake, drive north on NY 30 to Kickerville Road, which starts 0.6 miles past the bridge over the lake. Turn right and go 2.8 miles to a parking lot on the left. After parking, carry or wheel your boat 0.3 miles farther down the dirt road to a junction of three gated roads. Follow the leftmost road about 0.4 miles to the put-in. It's a short distance from the left side of the road.

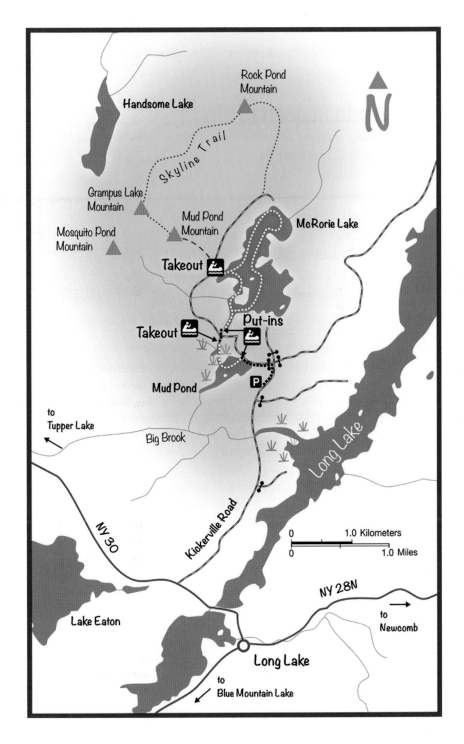

5. Axton to Raquette Falls

Length: 12 miles round-trip
Carries: None
Shuttle: No
Motors: Permitted
WSR status: Scenic
Meander quotient: 33%
Put-in: 44°12.209' N, 74°19.580' W
National Geographic map: Lake Placid/High Peaks

As the second-longest river in New York State, the Raquette River has something to offer every paddler from the raw beginner to the white-water junkie. For flatwater day-trippers, one of the best excursions is the twelve-mile round-trip from Axton Landing to Raquette Falls.

Axton Landing is the ideal put-in: a sandy strand in a sheltered cove. Its name comes from "Ax Town," a reminder of its logging past. Photos of Axton from the late 1800s show a denuded landscape. The tall pines found at Axton today were planted more than a century ago. It was the state's first forest plantation.

As you paddle across the small cove, look to the left for a grand view of the Seward Range in the High Peaks Wilderness. For most of the journey, the Raquette forms the western boundary of the Wilderness Area. On the other side of the river is Follensby Park, a 14,600-acre wild tract purchased by the Nature Conservancy in 2008 with the intention of reselling it to the state.

Despite the proximity of the Wilderness Area, where motorized use is forbidden, powerboats are allowed on this stretch of the Raquette. As you wind upstream, you'll see buoys meant to steer boaters away from shallows. Motorboats are supposed to travel no faster than five miles an hour, but not everyone obeys the speed limit.

Upon exiting the cove, turn left to go upriver. The current is sluggish most of the year, but during spring snowmelt it's considerably stronger. A half-mile from the put-in, you reach the grassy mouth of Stony Creek on the left, with a view of nearby peaks. Just beyond the stream is the first of three

Raquette Falls. Photo by Phil Brown

lean-tos between Axton and the falls.

Shortly after, you begin heading south but not in a straight line: the Raquette turns more often than a weathervane in a cyclone. If you were a crow, you'd need to travel only four miles, not six, to get to Raquette Falls. Shaggy-barked silver maples, a colonizer of floodplains, grow along the riverbanks for much of the route. The maple forest is open enough that in the high water of early spring it's possible to paddle among the trees and cut corners.

As you meander upriver, you'll pass a number of bays and inlets that invite exploration. Many of the detours lead to marshes where you might see herons or signs of beaver. You also can find plenty of birds without leaving the main river. Some of the more common are mallards, mergansers, belted kingfishers, red-eyed vireos, and white-throated sparrows.

At 5.4 miles, you reach the third lean-to, perched above a sandy bank. Soon after, you pass a cedar grove on the right and start to hear rapids. When you see the rapids, head toward a huge boulder near the east shore. Take out on a beach on the other side of the boulder.

Leave your boat on the beach to hike to the falls. Follow a herd path a few hundred feet to a junction with an old tote road, now used as a carry

View of the Seward Range from Axton. Photo by Phil Brown

trail. In the clearing ahead is a forest ranger's cabin. Turn right and walk a few hundred feet to another junction. Turn right again and follow a path a quarter-mile to the lower falls.

At the lower falls, the Raquette drops a dozen feet or so into a frothy kettle and then squeezes through a rocky channel. It's not the most dramatic cascade, but the bedrock on the shore is a good picnic place. The upper falls are about three-quarters of a mile upriver. Those who want to visit them can try to follow a faint path that starts here and parallels the river. Another option is to return to the tote road, turn right, and hike a mile to its end at a pool in the river. When you get there, look for a path that follows the river's right bank and follow it a quarter-mile to the upper falls. Although they are a bit larger than the lower falls, the view is not as good.

Before returning to Axton, stop at the ranger's cabin to find the boulder marking the grave of George Morgan, a woodsman who lived here from 1919 to 1944. It's in the northeast corner of the clearing. In the nineteenth century, the clearing was the site of a lodge run by Mother Johnson. Seneca Ray Stoddard tells of a mysterious fish she once served him. When he asked what kind of fish it was, she replied: "Well, they don't have no name after the fifteenth of September. They are a good deal like trout, but it's against the law to catch trout after the fifteenth, you know."

DIRECTIONS: From the traffic light near town hall in Saranac Lake, drive west on NY 3 for 12.7 miles to Coreys Road on the left (reached 4.5 miles past the parking lot for Ampersand Mountain). Go down Coreys Road for 1.9 miles to a rough access road on the right. Follow this road 0.2 miles to Axton Landing at the end.

6. Stony Creek Ponds & Raquette River

Length: 10.4 miles

Carries: 0.1 miles

Shuttle: 5.2 miles

Motors: Permitted

WSR status: Scenic

Meander quotient: 36%

Put-in: 44°13.325' N, 74°18.857' W

Takeout: 44°14.384' N, 74°23.315' W

National Geographic map: Lake Placid/High Peaks

Every spring, rains and melting snows combine to turn the silver-maple floodplain of Stony Creek and the Raquette River into a shallow lake. If you want the surreal experience of paddling in a forest, pick a warm day in April for this excursion. But it's an enjoyable trip anytime.

You start in the woodsy settlement of Coreys. A short path leads from the road to Third Pond, the smallest of the three Stony Creek Ponds (once known as Spectacle Ponds). Seasonal homes have been built on the shores, but after you leave the ponds behind, the only domiciles you see are lean-tos and beaver lodges.

From the put-in, it takes only a few minutes to paddle across the little pond into the larger Second Pond. Keep heading east until you see the channel on the right that leads to First Pond. Soon after entering the channel, you come to a wooden bridge. If the water is high, you have to carry around it. First Pond lies just beyond.

At 1.25 miles from the put-in, you reach the end of the ponds and the start of the outlet. As you leave First Pond, look for Ampersand Brook on the left. If you have time, you can paddle a mile upstream (you may encounter deadfalls). As you paddle down Stony Creek, take note of the hand-dug channel to the left; it was once used to float logs to the Raquette.

Most of the year Stony Creek winds through a forest of silver maples. In the last half of April, it knows no boundaries. You can cut corners by leaving the main channel and paddling through the forest (not that cutting corners is

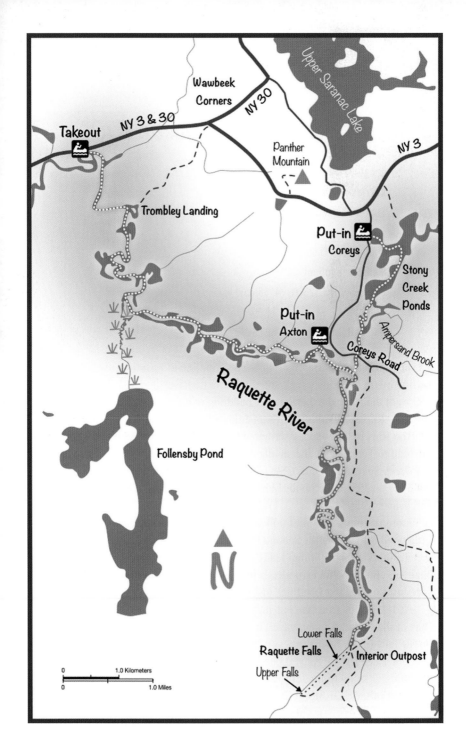

Weaving among Stony Creek's silver maples. Photo by Mark Bowie

the point). At 2.3 miles from the put-in, you reach Coreys Road, which leads to trails in the High Peaks Wilderness. Again, you may have to carry around the bridge in high water.

At 2.7 miles, after winding through grasses, Stony Creek enters the Raquette. Turn right to head downriver. In a quarter-mile, you come to a cable that hunters use to cross the Raquette. Most of the time, the cable is high above the water, but during spring floods, you may need to duck beneath it. Soon after you pass Axton Landing on the right, the starting point for the trip to Raquette Falls. Turn into the little bay for a nice view of the Sewards in the east. The river becomes more meandering below Axton. Here, too, you'll be able to paddle among silver maples during the spring flood.

About 3.5 miles below Axton you reach the wide mouth of Follensby Pond's outlet. In 2008, the Adirondack Chapter of the Nature Conservancy bought the large pond and surrounding lands with the intention of selling the whole tract—some 14,600 acres—to the state. Once in the Forest Pre- serve, Follensby Pond is sure to become a popular destination for paddlers. Until then, it's off limits. Meantime, feel free to explore the marshy outlet. After another three miles of meandering, the Raquette passes Trombley Landing, where a lean-to sits among pines on a sandy bluff. This is a good

The mouth of Follensby Pond's outlet. Photo by Phil Brown

spot to take a swim in the summer. There is a second lean-to in a backwater just to the east. There also are numerous campsites along the river where you can stop for a snack or swim.

From Trombley Landing, you have less than a mile and a half to go to reach the takeout at the state boat launch, known locally as the Crusher. You will have paddled at least 10.4 miles—more if you explored the Follensby Pond outlet or the many sloughs along the river. From the takeout, it's a 5.2-mile bike ride or drive back to the starting point.

DIRECTIONS: From the intersection of NY 3 and Main Street in Saranac Lake, drive west on NY 3 for about 12 miles and take note of Coreys Road on the left. Continue on NY 3 for three miles to Wawbeek Corners. Bear left onto NY 3/30 and go 1.6 miles to the state boat launch on the left. This is the takeout. For the put-in, return to Coreys Road, turn right, and go 0.6 miles to the start of a carry trail on the left.

7. Middle & Lower Saranac Lakes

Length of trip: 6 to 12.5 miles
Carries: 20 yards at lock
Shuttle: 5.8 miles
Motors: Permitted
WSR status: Recreational
Put-in: 44°14.671' N, 74°16.125' W
Takeout: 44°17.297' N, 74°11.110' W
National Geographic map: Lake Placid/High Peaks

In 1931, after years of fighting tuberculosis, Martha Reben sought to cure herself by going into the wilderness. With guide Fred Rice, the young woman camped for five months on Weller Pond. She did regain a measure of health and wrote a book, *The Healing Woods*, in which she extols the virtues of outdoor living. Although the TB era has passed, Weller Pond is still good medicine for the soul.

Weller is a secluded adjunct of Middle Saranac Lake. Rice and Reben reached Weller by way of Lower Saranac Lake and the Saranac River. On the trip described here, you can retrace most of their route, but in reverse. All of Weller Pond and most of Middle Saranac and Lower Saranac belong to the Forest Preserve. The state maintains eighty-seven campsites, including five lean-tos, on the shorelines and islands of these beautiful waters. Collectively, the sites make up the Saranac Lake Islands Campground; a fee is charged for overnight stays from late May until early October (reservations required).

Your journey begins on South Creek, an inlet of Middle Saranac, and ends at the campground headquarters on Route 3. The state maintains a launch site for car-top boats on South Creek. As you travel downstream, take the time to observe the variety of wetland plants, such as leatherleaf, sundew, bog rosemary, black spruce, and tamarack. In 0.4 miles, you come to the lake, with Boot Bay Mountain rising straight ahead.

Middle Saranac sees far fewer motorboats than Lower Saranac, in part because of its isolation. Powerboaters can go from Lower to Middle via the Saranac River, but they must pass through a lock and obey a five-mile-an-hour speed limit on the winding stream. Nonetheless, some boaters make the upriver trip to loll on the beach on Middle Saranac's south shore or to fish in Weller Pond.

When you reach Middle Saranac from South Creek, paddle due north. The lake is relatively shallow and gets choppy in a breeze. As you cross, take in the views of Ampersand Mountain to the south and McKenzie and Whiteface mountains to the east. After passing Halfway Island, angle left to enter Hungry Bay. Stay close to the right shore of the bay, round Rice Point, and look for Weller's outlet in the bay's northeast corner, reached 1.9 miles from the put-in.

Like South Creek, the outlet flows through an attractive wetland. The stream is only a quarter-mile long. Shortly before reaching Weller Pond, look for a weedy channel on the right that leads to Little Weller Pond at the base of Boot Bay Mountain. The short detour to this little gem is worthwhile. Reben and Rice also camped on Little Weller.

Weller Pond is much larger than its sidekick: nearly a mile in length. At the west end is a lean-to dedicated to Reben. Actually, the patient and her guide had set up residence on the north shore of the pond on what is now known as Reben Point. One of the state campsites (No. 85) occupies the same spot. There are three other tent sites on Weller, including one on Tick Island, a big island near the middle of the pond (a smaller one to its north is sometimes called Toc).

Wild and serene, Weller Pond is a destination in itself and can be visited in a six-mile round-trip from South Creek. But more delights await those who do the through trip to Lower Saranac. Upon returning to Middle Saranac, head east and stay close to the north shore. As you approach the end of the lake, you'll find buoys marking a channel in the reeds. This is the lake's outlet, the Saranac River.

The river winds through a beautiful marshland, adorned in summer with blooms of pickerelweed and water lilies. It's one of the highlights of the trip. After 1.4 miles on the river, you arrive at a manual lock near a small rapid. State workers operate the lock in summer; in the off-season, boaters can operate it themselves by following the instructions. If you're paddling, it's quicker to carry around the lock.

Below the lock the shoreline is mostly wooded, but after another half-mile or so, you'll see a marshy area on the left. This is Kelly Slough, a quiet backwater worth poking into. A little beyond the slough, a rock precipice overlooks the entrance to Lower Saranac Lake.

Kelly Slough off the Saranac River. Photo by Phil Brown

Bluff Island on Lower Saranac. Photo by Susan Bibeau

As you reach the lake, McKenzie Mountain comes into view again.

With its many islands and mountain views, Lower Saranac is among the loveliest of Adirondack lakes. However, you must be prepared to share it with a fair number of motorboats, especially in summer. Paddle northeast to the Narrows, passing Loon Bay on the right, and continue in the same general direction. After two miles, you'll be approaching Bluff Island, with its conspicuous seventy-foot cliffs. Available for day use, the island is a nice place to picnic or swim. If you're not stopping, though, turn right and follow a marked channel to First Pond. After passing under Route 3, take out at the state-owned docks on the right. The through trip, including a visit to Weller, is about 12.5 miles.

Incidentally, Martha Reben wrote two more books and lived to be fifty-three. She died in 1964, and Fred Rice passed away two years later. Their ashes were scattered at Weller Pond.

DIRECTIONS: From the traffic light at the intersection of NY 3 and Main Street in downtown Saranac Lake, drive west on NY 3 for 4.2 miles to the boat launch and campground entrance on the left. This is the takeout. For the put-in, drive another 5.8 miles to the South Creek boat launch on the left.

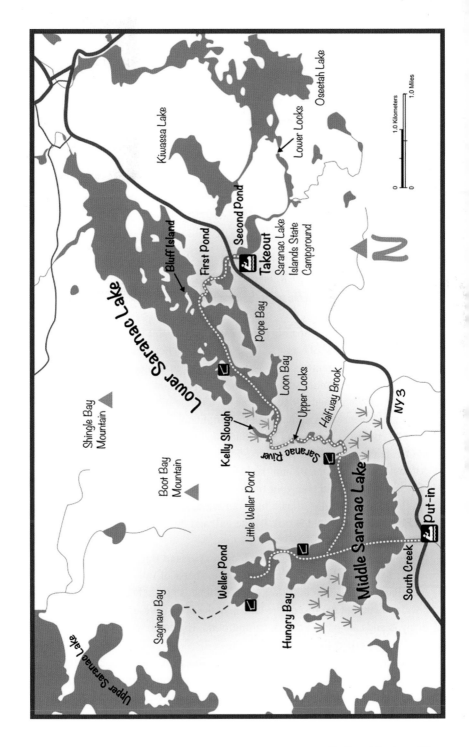

Oseetah Lake

Kiwassa Lake

Lower Locks

Second Pond

First Pond

Bluff Island

Lower Saranac Lake

Takeout
Saranac Lake
Islands State
Campground

Pope Bay

Loon Bay

Upper Locks

Shingle Bay
Mountain

Halfway Brook

Kelly Slough

Saranac River

NY 3

Boot Bay
Mountain

Little Weller Pond

Middle Saranac Lake

Put-in

Weller Pond

South Creek

Saginaw Bay

Hungry Bay

Upper Saranac Lake

1.0 Kilometers

1.0 Miles

N

8. Round the Mountain Loop

Length: Up to 13.5 miles

Carries: 100 yards

Shuttle: 1.6 miles

Motors: Permitted

WSR status: Recreational

Put-in: 44°19.552' N, 74°09.289' W

Takeout: 44°19.410' N, 74°07.515' W

National Geographic maps: Saranac/Paul Smiths, Lake Placid/High Peaks

Dewey Mountain is not a big peak (2,050 feet), but it looms large in the life of the village of Saranac Lake, thanks to a network of popular trails that attract cross-country skiers and snowshoers in winter and hikers and mountain bikers in other seasons. Dewey is also known to paddlers: the Adirondack Watershed Alliance sponsors a canoe race each spring in which participants nearly circumnavigate the mountain.

The contestants start on Lower Saranac Lake, follow the Saranac River to Oseetah Lake, and finish on Lake Flower in the heart of the village. Although racing is fun, it's not the best way to enjoy the scenery. So come back another day and take your time. If you stick to the official racecourse, you'll get in 10.5 miles of paddling, but we suggest adding short side trips up Fish Creek and Cold Brook. These will add three miles at most to the excursion.

You start at a car-top boat launch on Ampersand Bay at the east end of Lower Saranac Lake, one of most beautiful sheets of water in the Adirondack Park. The eastern third of Lower Saranac is privately owned, with some development, but the rest of the lake is in the Forest Preserve. Most of its many islands are part of a state campground. Expect to share the lake with motorboats, especially in summer.

After launching, stay close to the north shore. In a mile, look for the mouth of Fish Creek on the right. This sluggish stream teems with pickerel-weed and water lilies and is a haven for ducks and herons. You can paddle

Oseetah Lake with McKenzie Mountain in background. Photo by Phil Brown

about a mile upstream. Returning to the lake, you have a good view of Dewey Mountain.

A half-mile beyond Fish Creek, you pass the boathouse and camps of Knollwood, a private compound where Bob Marshall, the legendary wilderness advocate, spent his boyhood summers. Marshall and his brother, George, with their guide, Herb Clark, were the first hikers to climb all the Adirondack peaks over four thousand feet. Bob may have been inspired by the impressive views of mountains enjoyed from this part of the lake.

After passing Knollwood, head south and thread your way among the islands to Bluff Island. On the island's south side, a cliff rises seventy feet out of the lake. On a hot summer day, you may see people jumping into the water. From the cliff, you should be able to discern a wide channel a little to the south. This is the Saranac River.

Follow the channel through First Pond (a broadening of the river), under the Route 3 bridge, and past the boat launch for the Saranac Lake Islands State Campground. The river widens again to form Second Pond, with views of the western High Peaks. Beyond Second Pond, the river narrows and flows through wild forest. Numerous buoys mark the channel for motorboats.

At 1.2 miles from Route 3 (or 5.5 miles from the put-in), you come to a lean-to on the left bank. Either the lean-to or the enormous boulders sitting in the water a bit downriver would make a good lunch spot. If you land near the boulders and walk a short distance into the woods, you'll find an extensive boulder field.

Just beyond the riverside boulders is a marsh where Cold Brook enters from the right. You can paddle a half-mile up this peaceful stream before blowdown blocks the way. It's a pleasant diversion from the sometimes-busy Saranac.

After joining forces with Cold Brook, the Saranac passes through a drowned land of stumps, pickerelweed, and water lilies and in a half-mile reaches a lock at a small dam. You can pass through the lock or follow a carry trail around the dam. The trail begins at a dock on the right.

On the other side of the dam, the river morphs into Oseetah Lake. Unlike Lower Saranac, nearly all of Oseetah is privately owned, and it has many more camps. Despite the many camps and motorboat traffic, Oseetah is a beautiful lake, with knockout views of peaks near and far, including the McKenzie Range and Whiteface Mountain.

For the shortest route to the village, stay to the left, near the grassy shallows, upon entering the lake. Head northeast toward some islands at the beginning of a channel that leads to a part of lake bordered by Oseetah Marsh. You change course, heading northwest to enter another channel, this one leading to Lake Flower. As you paddle into the village, you re-enter the world of cars, marinas, motels, and houses. The takeout at the state boat launch is on the north shore near a grassy park.

If you have time, Pine Pond is another delightful side trip. It can be reached by a half-mile stroll along old woods roads, starting from Oseetah's southernmost bay. Head up the main road, then bear right at the first junction, left at the second. You soon arrive at a sandy beach. The clear water invites swimming, but the pond is not large enough to warrant bringing along your boat.

DIRECTIONS: The takeout is at the large state boat launch on Lake Flower in the village of Saranac Lake. The launch's entrance is on the south side of NY 86. To reach the put-in, turn left after exiting the parking lot and go straight for 1.1 miles to Edgewood Road (just past the school on the right). Turn right and go 0.3 miles to Bayside Drive. Turn left and go 0.2 miles to a launch on Lower Saranac Lake for car-top boats.

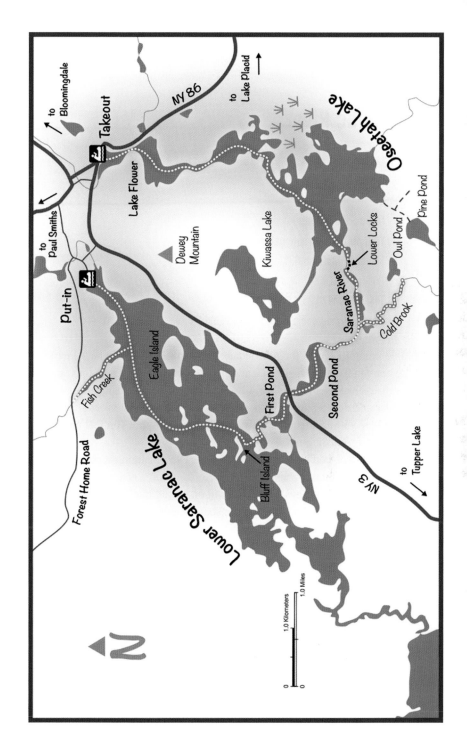

9. Saranac River

Length: 10.7 miles

Carries: None

Shuttle: 9.6 miles

Motors: Permitted

WSR status: Recreational

Meander quotient: 23%

Put-in: 44°19.847' N, 74°07.575' W

Takeout: 44°24.253' N, 74°01.923' W

National Geographic map: Saranac/Paul Smiths

People unfamiliar with the Adirondack Park's history wonder how a park can contain hamlets, highways, and private lands. Well, it just does, and the Saranac River exemplifies the Adirondacks' peculiar juxtaposition of wilderness and development. You start this trip in the village of Saranac Lake and stay within earshot of Route 3 for much of it, but you feel closer to nature than to civilization.

On a clear day, you're sure to delight in the ever-changing scenery, especially the breathtaking vista of the McKenzie Range near the mouth of Moose Creek. On most days, you can count on seeing ducks, mergansers, and herons. If you're lucky, you may see something more unusual, such as a bald eagle, black bear, or even a moose.

You can put in either at the Pine Street bridge or at the Riverwalk ramp near the Dorsey Street parking lot. If you begin at the ramp, add a half-mile to the trip and know that you'll encounter riffles as you approach Pine Street. Keep to the right in the riffles if the water is low.

Most of the development along the river occurs early on. Within a few miles of Pine Street, the Saranac flows under power lines twice and past a sewage-treatment plant. At 1.75 miles, just past the second set of power lines, there is a good view of Baker Mountain, a favorite among local hikers. If you climb Baker, you'll enjoy a reciprocal view of the Saranac River valley. (The trail starts near Moody Pond in the village.)

A little farther on, you pass a sluggish inlet on the left and soon come

View of the McKenzie Range from a tributary of the Saranac River. Photo by Phil Brown

to a vista of slide-scarred Moose Mountain, the tallest peak in the McKenzie Range. Eventually, the whole ridge between Moose and McKenzie Mountain comes into view. Both peaks rise to almost 3,900 feet—more than 2,400 feet above the valley.

At 2.75 miles you arrive at the mouth of Moose Creek, though it might be hard to find with all the marshy channels. You can paddle up the creek about a half-mile. It's worth going up at least a little way: the scene of the creek meandering through grasses and pickerelweed with the mountains in the background is not to be missed.

The forest along the Saranac is ever shifting from hardwoods to conifers to a mixture of both. Just below Moose Creek, silver maples dominate the floodplain. In spring, when the water is high, you can leave the main channel to weave between these water-tolerant trees.

At 4.5 miles, you come to a green bridge, the start of a mile-long trail that leads to Moose Pond. If you have time, you might want to take a walk to this large pond: it's surrounded by Forest Preserve, and the west shore offers views of the McKenzie Range and Whiteface Mountain.

A half-mile beyond the bridge, the river starts to meander more, alternately pulling near and away from Route 3. At 5.2 miles, it passes under a low bridge that's privately owned. If the water is high, you'll have to carry around it. Eventually, the Saranac veers away from Route 3 for good and

A lazy downstream trip on the Saranac. Photo by Phil Brown

enters a large alder swamp. At 6.9 miles, Sumner Brook enters from the left. Shortly, you start to see homes and camps on the left side of the river. From the mouth of Cold Brook, you enjoy a good view of the slide on the west flank of Moose Mountain.

At 8.5 miles, you paddle beneath the bridge at Moose Pond Road and soon pass several seasonal camps near the water. The river continues to meander through alders for a while but straightens out as it enters an evergreen corridor. At 10.7 miles, just after riding through some riffles, take out on the left along River Road before the start of Permanent Rapids. There is a Northern Forest Canoe Trail marker at the takeout. The entire river, from the Saranac Lakes to Lake Champlain, is on the NFCT.

Belted kingfisher. Photo by Jeff Nadler

DIRECTIONS: The Dorsey Street parking lot lies between Main Street and the river in the village of Saranac Lake. The wooden boat ramp is easily found from the lot. The Pine Street bridge is near Pine Street's junction with NY 3. To reach the takeout, turn right from Pine Street onto NY 3 and go 6.3 miles to the four-way intersection in Bloomingdale. Turn right and go 0.2 miles to River Road. Turn right and go 3.1 miles to the takeout on the right. Look for the Northern Forest Canoe Trail marker.

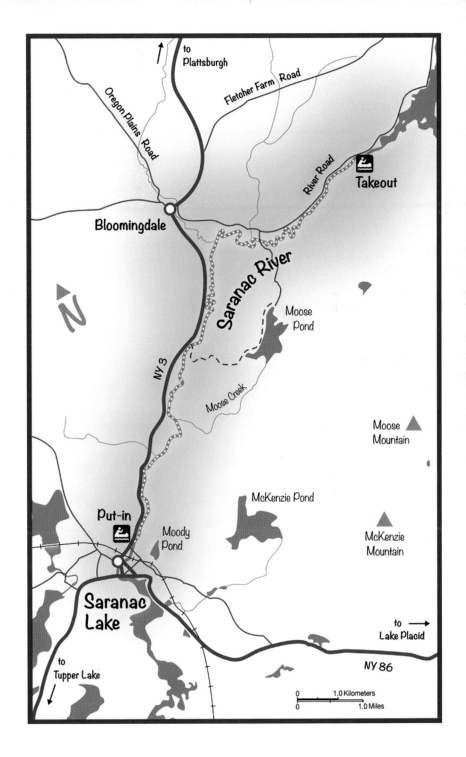

to
Plattsburgh

Oregon Plains Road

Fletcher Farm Road

River Road

Takeout

Bloomingdale

Saranac River

Moose Pond

NY 3

Moose Creek

Moose Mountain

McKenzie Pond

Put-in

Moody Pond

McKenzie Mountain

Saranac Lake

to
Lake Placid

NY 86

to
Tupper Lake

0   1.0 Kilometers
0   1.0 Miles

Heading up the Chubb River, with Nye Mountain on the horizon. Photo by Phil Brown

10. Chubb River

Length: 8 miles round-trip
Carries: 2 totaling 450 yards
Shuttle: No
Motors: Prohibited
Meander quotient: 33%
Put-in: 44°15.726' N, 74°01.022' W
National Geographic map: Lake Placid/High Peaks

With its steep terrain and rocky streams, the High Peaks Wilderness is not the domain of paddlers. Those who want to penetrate this magnificent region by boat have only one easy option: the Chubb River.

From the put-in outside Lake Placid, paddlers can travel about four miles up the river, eventually reaching a vast marsh with impressive vistas of mountains. Visitors also can expect to see a variety of birds. Besides red-winged blackbirds, white-throated sparrows, and the usual waterfowl, boreal species such as black-backed woodpecker, Lincoln's sparrow, and boreal chickadee dwell along the Chubb.

The put-in is on a stillwater just above a short stretch of rapids. Paddling upriver, you wind through alders. Lily pads dot the stream in summer. Evergreen trees line the banks: balsam fir, red spruce, tamarack, northern white cedar, and the occasional white pine rising above them all.

It's all wild until you reach a house and small dock at 0.7 miles—the only signs of civilization on the entire trip. Just beyond the house, the alders close in so that it seems as though you're paddling through a tunnel, but the river soon widens again.

Almost a mile from the put-in is a large beaver dam. As you pull your boat over or around it, you'll probably hear rapids ahead—the start of a three-hundred-yard carry, reached at 1.1 miles. Take out at a grassy bank on the left to follow a marked portage trail. About halfway up the trail there is a campsite on the left.

Above the next put-in, the river meanders up the valley between the

Sawtooth Range to the southwest and Nye and Street mountains to the southeast. The Chubb originates in a vly between Nye and Street, which are familiar to hikers as two of the forty-six High Peaks. After rounding the first bend, look for the slide scars on Nye. Many of the High Peaks have similar scars, created by rainstorms that washed away the soil and vegetation. Nye's slides are unusual in that they were caused by an earthquake.

Farther upstream, the views of surrounding peaks expand as you venture deeper into the Chubb River Marsh, a lush wetland recognized by the Adirondack Park Agency as an extraordinary natural area. After a mile or so from the carry, be sure to look back for a view of Whiteface Mountain, the state's fifth-highest peak.

Lincoln's sparrow Photo by Larry Master

How far you travel up the Chubb will depend on the water level and your stamina. In spring, you can paddle four miles or more before the stream constricts to make further passage impractical. Expect to pull your boat over several beaver dams along the way. You may be able to ride over some of the dams on the return trip. In late spring and early summer, you also can expect to encounter black flies, so pack bug dope.

Putting up with a few dams and a few hundred insects is a small price to pay for seeing firsthand the beauty and birdlife of the Chubb. As Paul Jamieson wrote: "Weaving through the marsh in an amphitheater of mountains is an unforgettable experience."

DIRECTIONS: From Old Military Road on the outskirts of Lake Placid village, drive south on Averyville Road. After crossing the Chubb at 1.1 miles, continue 0.2 miles and, after cresting a small hill, look for the carry trail on the left. There is a small "State Land" sign on a tree at the start. Park along the shoulder.

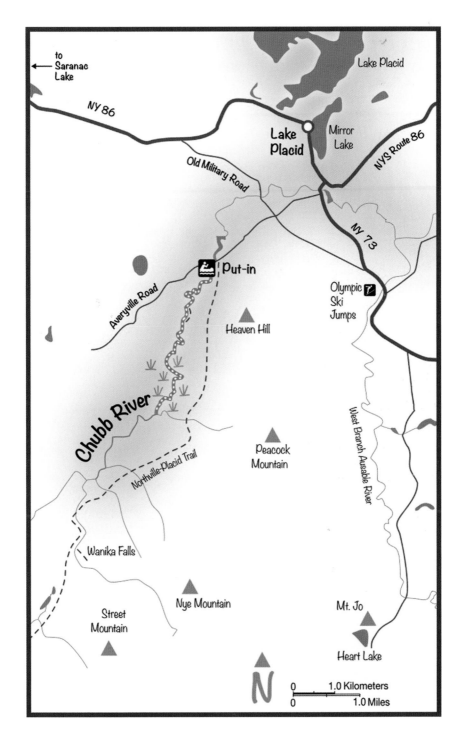

to Saranac Lake

NY 86

Lake Placid

Lake Placid

Mirror Lake

NYS Route 86

Old Military Road

NY 73

Put-in

Averyville Road

Heaven Hill

Olympic Ski Jumps

Chubb River

Northville-Placid Trail

Peacock Mountain

West Branch Ausable River

Wanika Falls

Nye Mountain

Mt. Jo

Street Mountain

Heart Lake

N

0   1.0 Kilometers
0   1.0 Miles

The West Branch of the Ausable. Photo by Ray Palmer

11. West Branch of the Ausable

Length: 5.4 miles

Carries: 0.2 miles

Shuttle: 4.1 miles

Motors: Permitted

WSR status: Recreational

Meander quotient: 35%

Put-in: 44°16.028' N, 73°57.047' W

Takeout: 44°18.638' N, 73°54.940' W

National Geographic maps: Lake Placid/High Peaks, Saranac/Paul Smiths

The West Branch of the Ausable on the outskirts of Lake Placid is famed among fly fishermen but often overlooked by paddlers. If you're looking for a fun, scenic cruise that can be done in a morning or an afternoon, leaving time to see the Olympic sites, this is a good choice.

This stretch of the West Branch has a few shallow riffles, so if you're worried about scratching your boat, it's best paddled in spring or after a good rain. That said, this excursion usually can be done anytime in summer or fall without much trouble.

From the put-in off River Road, you can travel 5.4 miles downriver to Monument Falls off Route 86. The one carry, around rapids, can be avoided by ending your trip at the Route 86 bridge instead of continuing to the falls. You'll need to spot a second car or bicycle at whichever takeout you choose.

Although the river is never far from roads, you stand a good chance of seeing wild birds such as mallards, mergansers, and herons on the water. The guidebook *Adirondack Birding* says a variety of other birds can be found in the vicinity of the river, including northern species such as boreal chickadee, black-backed woodpecker, and ruby-crowned kinglet.

You'll also find impressive views. After launching, look to the east to see the Sentinel Range, whose highest peaks, Kilburn and Sentinel, surpass 3,800 feet. As you head downriver, turn around once in a while to take in the High Peaks to the south. At times you'll also enjoy views of Whiteface Mountain to the northeast.

The West Branch, with a partial view of the Sentinel Range. Photo by Phil Brown

The river winds through woods and past fields. At 1.0 mile, as the river draws close to the road, you pass the first of several homes constructed on the right bank. At 2.7 miles, you are treated to an excellent view of White-face. At 3.5 miles, the Ausable flows under Route 86. If you want to avoid the carry ahead, take out on the left on the downstream side of the bridge. Even if you choose to pull out here, you should first continue a quarter-mile beyond the bridge to take in a superb view of the Sentinel Range. It's an easy paddle back upstream to Route 86.

The carry starts 0.8 miles beyond the bridge. Shortly before this, the river pulls away from Route 86. As you round a right bend, you may hear water rushing through a breached dam and small gorge. Be sure to take out before the dam. A rough path on the right bank leads in 0.2 miles to calm water. If you feel comfortable in whitewater, you may want to scout the class II rapids below the gorge to see if they're navigable.

Below the rapids, the river sidles close to Route 86 and then pulls away again. Rounding the next bend, you find yourself on a straightaway with a spectacular view of Whiteface. When the river turns right again, keep your ears open for water spilling over Monument Falls. Take out on the right just before the drop.

DIRECTIONS: From the intersection of NY 73 and NY 86 in Lake Placid, drive 4.3 miles east on 86 to the Monument Falls pull-off on the left. This is the takeout. To reach the put-in, head back toward Lake Placid on NY 86 for 1.1 miles to River Road. Turn left and go 2.1 miles to a pull-off on the right next to the Intervale Road bridge.

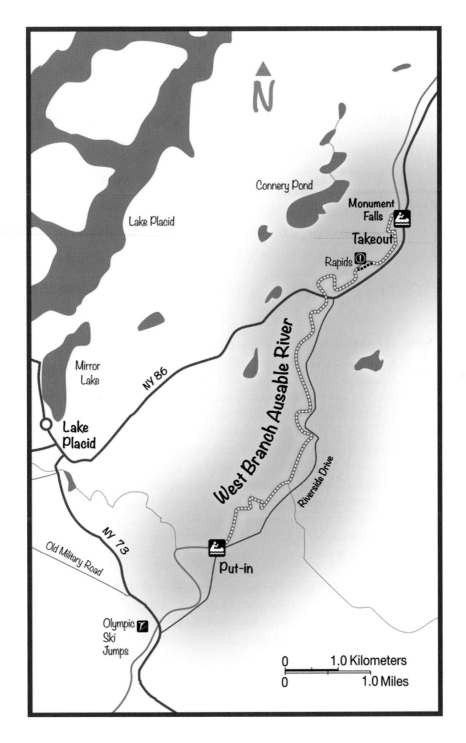

N

Connery Pond

Lake Placid

Monument
Falls

Takeout

Rapids

Lake Placid

Mirror
Lake

NY 86

West Branch Ausable River

Lake
Placid

Riverside Drive

NY 73

Old Military Road

Put-in

Olympic
Ski
Jumps

0   1.0 Kilometers
0   1.0 Miles

12. Jones Pond, Osgood Pond & Osgood River

Length: Up to 10 miles

Carries: None

Shuttle: Optional

Motors: Permitted

WSR status: Study River

Jones Pond put-in: 44°27.426' N, 74°11.336' W

Church Pond takeout: 44°26.366' N, 74°14.936' W

National Geographic map: Saranac/Paul Smiths

This trip can be done in various permutations, some shorter, some longer, but if you want to experience the full diversity of scenery, flora, birdlife, and historical curiosities, you need to paddle the whole thing, starting at Jones Pond and taking out at Church Pond. If you don't have a second car, leave a bicycle at the takeout; it's only a twenty-minute pedal back to Jones Pond.

The put-in is on Forest Preserve along the northern bay of Jones Pond. If you have to drive a long distance to get here, you may want to spend a night at one of the primitive campsites amid the pines. There also are two campsites on the pond's northwestern shore and one on the southern shore.

After launching, paddle west toward the outlet. In less than a half-mile, you come to a lush marsh teeming with cattails, bulrushes, water lilies, pickerelweed, and other aquatic plants. You may want to explore the braided channels that penetrate the marsh, a refuge for ducks, bitterns, coots, and other waterfowl.

Beyond the marsh, the outlet passes under County Route 31 and winds through an evergreen forest that's home to boreal birds such as the black-backed woodpecker and gray jay. Also listen for warblers and look for turtles sunning themselves on logs. Expect to see a few beaver dams. If the water is low, you may have to pull your boat over them.

About a mile from the highway, the sluggish stream passes under a second bridge, on White Pine Road, and soon after empties into Osgood Pond near a sandy beach. A bald eagle sometimes perches in a white pine at the mouth.

Paddling past evergreen spires on the Osgood River. Photo by Phil Brown

Osgood Pond can be choppy in a breeze. Paddle northwest toward a small building at the end of a point (as you get closer, you'll see it's actually on a little island connected to the mainland by an arched footbridge). This is the Japanese tea house at White Pine Camp. Constructed in 1907-08, White Pine Camp served as the "Summer White House" for President Calvin Coolidge in 1926. It's now a woodsy resort open to the public.

The Osgood River, the pond's outlet, starts roughly a half-mile beyond the teahouse. Entering the Osgood, you can look straight downriver at Debar Mountain, one of the larger peaks in this part of the Park. As you paddle on, you'll see an open sedge mat on the west side of the river—a habitat similar to Canadian muskeg. On the east side of the river is a black-spruce swamp.

American three-toed woodpecker, one of the rarest birds in the Adirondacks, has been spotted along the first mile of the river. Other northern species found on the Osgood include the boreal chickadee, palm warbler, Lincoln's sparrow, and black-backed woodpecker. Broad-winged hawks sometimes soar above.

A mile and a half from the pond, the Osgood winds among large patches of pickerelweed—a purple riot in late summer—and takes a sharp left. Blind Brook, a narrow tributary, enters from the right here. If you have time, it's worth exploring.

You can paddle the Osgood as far as the remnants of a stone-and-timber dam. If you do go this far, you will have traveled two and a half miles from Osgood Pond and nearly six miles from the put-in at Jones Pond. Beyond the old dam, the river is not navigable for long.

It's time to turn around. When you get back to Osgood Pond, head south to round the big point on the right and then head southwest, in the general direction of St. Regis Mountain (the one with the fire tower) and an island off the tip of another point. While crossing the lake, keep your eyes and ears open for common loons—as well as for that eagle. As you near the island, keep it on the right and bear left to enter a small bay.

Your journey is almost over. Look for a tiny canal that starts on the west side of the bay and follow it to Little Church Pond. Halfway across this pond, turn left to follow another canal to Church Pond. These charming canals, shaded by dark hemlocks, were dug by hand around 1900 so the summer residents of Osgood Pond could paddle or row to church in Paul Smiths. Paddle up Church Pond to your takeout, a wooden dock on the south shore along Route 86.

Palm warbler Photo by Larry Master

The ten-mile excursion can be shortened by starting at one of three optional put-ins—at either of the two bridges over the Jones Pond outlet or at a state launch site on Osgood Pond—and skipping part of the trip. But it'd be hard to decide what to miss.

DIRECTIONS: The Church Pond takeout is along NY 86, just east of that highway's junction with NY 30 in Paul Smiths. To reach Jones Pond from the takeout, drive 0.7 miles east on NY 86, turn left onto County 31, and go 2.5 miles to the put-in on the right.

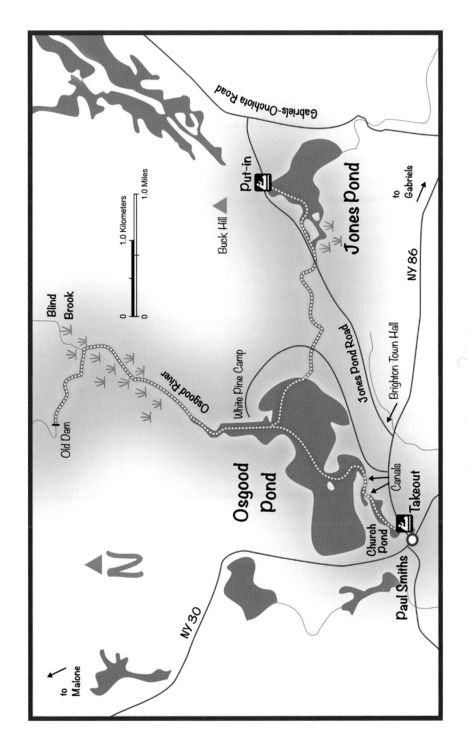

13. Lower Osgood River

Length: 9 miles

Carries: 1 (up to 0.4 miles)

Shuttle: 5.5 miles

Motors: Permitted

WSR status: Study River

Meander quotient: 39%

Put-in: 44°29.060' N, 74°16.915' W

Takeout: 44°33.221' N, 74°18.512' W

National Geographic map: Saranac Lake/Paul Smiths

Paul Jamieson once wrote that "only a fanatic" would try to pursue the Osgood River through the wetland thickets that lurk below its first navigable stretch. Tupper Lake's Bill Frenette was such a fanatic, and he reported that at one point the river vanished: "It goes down a hole like the last water from the tub." Paddlers should be thankful that the Osgood does reappear. A downstream cruise of the lower Osgood is one of the more varied and charming river trips in the Adirondacks.

There are several put-in options. If you don't mind a carry, the best place to start is the loop road used to access Mountain Pond and the Hays Brook Truck Trail. From the parking area, you may be able drive down a grassy lane for 0.3 miles to a turnaround where you can drop off your boat. From there it's maybe 150 yards to the river via a narrow path. The grassy lane is sometimes blocked by fallen trees, so you may have to carry the whole distance. Even if you can drive to the turnaround, you should not park there—which means you'll be walking from the parking area to the river one way or the other, either with or without your canoe.

At the put-in, the channel is narrow and shallow, partly clogged by overhanging alders. A mild current carries you along at the start, but it soon dies down. Within the first mile, you're likely to encounter blowdown and beaver dams.

Jamieson praised the lower Osgood as "unsurpassed in variety of riverine scenery," and the first piece of evidence for this claim is the piney

Quiet water near the takeout. Photo by Phil Brown

slope near the put-in. It's one of a series of eskers—narrow ridges of glacial sand and gravel—that border the river on its course to Meacham Lake.

Though constantly turning, the river generally heads northwest at first, pulling near Route 30 in several places. At 2.0 miles, near the hidden mouth of Hays Brook, it comes within ten yards of the highway and then veers away for good. On the east side of the Osgood, the outlets of three ponds cut through eskers and flow into the river. All three ponds are worth a visit, either by climbing over the eskers or, if possible, paddling up the short outlets (which are easy to miss).

The first is McCollums Pond. You reach its esker roughly a half-mile after the river turns away from the highway. Look for a good takeout a bit farther on. Baker Pond, perhaps the prettiest of the three, lies less than a half-mile north of McColloms, as the crow flies, but it's closer to a mile as the canoer plies. En route you pass a camp on the west shore and a footbridge. If you miss Baker's outlet, look for a primitive tent site on the esker. You can climb the ridge from there.

Mud Pond, the smallest, is reached in another half-mile or so. On the way you see more signs of development along the river: a cable, a ram-shackle wooden bridge, and a camp with another bridge. Mud's outlet is a quarter-mile past the second bridge.

Soon after leaving Mud, you pass another camp and bridge, the last development until the takeout. As you approach Meacham Lake, the Osgood meanders through a broad wetland—a mix of coniferous swamp, deciduous shrub swamp, and emergent marsh—with views of Debar Mountain in the north. You might see northern birds here, such as gray jay and boreal chickadee.

At 7.5 miles, you arrive at Meacham Lake, the second-largest Adirondack lake (after Lila) completely surrounded by Forest Preserve. Unless you're staying at the state campground on the other end, you needn't worry about crossing it. Turn west and hug the south shore. In about a half-mile you'll reach

Gray jay Photo by Larry Master

the lake's outlet, the East Branch of the St. Regis. Follow this channel for another half-mile or so, winding among pickerelweed and water lilies, to the takeout on the right. Those who don't want to bother with a shuttle can do a round-trip from here.

Paddlers looking for a slightly longer trip can start at a bridge over the Osgood on the Hays Brook Truck Trail. It requires a 0.4-mile carry.

DIRECTIONS: From the junction of NY 30 and NY 86 in Paul Smiths, drive 9.3 miles north on NY 30 to a parking area on the north side of the outlet of Meacham Lake. The turn is 0.25 miles north of NY 458. This is the takeout. To reach the put-in, head back on NY 30 toward Paul Smiths for 5.6 miles. Turn left at the DEC sign for the Hays Brook area and go 0.3 miles to a parking area on the left. A grassy lane leads from the parking area to turnaround where you can drop off your boat, but don't leave your car there.

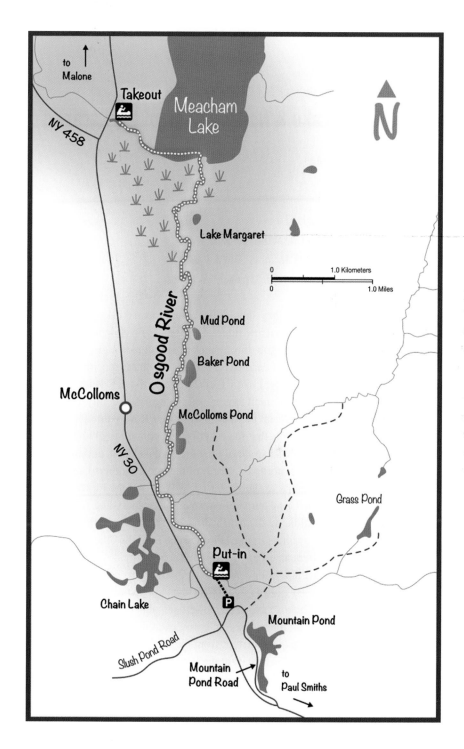

to
Malone

Takeout

Meacham
Lake

NY 458

N

Lake Margaret

0   1.0 Kilometers

0   1.0 Miles

Osgood River

Mud Pond

Baker Pond

McColloms

McColloms Pond

NY 30

Grass Pond

Put-in

P

Chain Lake

Mountain Pond

Slush Pond Road

Mountain
Pond Road

to
Paul Smiths

14. Rainbow Lake & North Branch of the Saranac

Length: 11 miles
Carries: 0.2 miles
Shuttle: 5.5 miles
Motors: Permitted
Put-in: 44°30.160' N, 74°07.700' W
Takeout: 44°27.708' N, 74°11.230' W
National Geographic map: Saranac/Paul Smiths

Since paddlers like rivers, they should like eskers too. An esker (the word comes from Ireland) is a narrow ridge of sand and gravel deposited in the ice age by streams running on, through, or beneath glaciers. Essentially, then, an esker is the bones of a dead river. Perhaps the finest specimen in the Adirondacks is the Rainbow Lake Esker. The geologist A.F. Buddington believed it was once part of a much longer esker that snaked eighty-five miles across the Adirondacks, all the way to Stillwater Reservoir.

What matters on this trip is that the esker is long enough to divide Rainbow Lake in two. The lake south of the esker is developed, and in summer it gets busy with motorboats. North of the esker paddlers can find refuge in two tranquil waterways known as Clear Pond and the Flow.

But the high point on this excursion—for both its scenery and serenity—has to be the paddle up the North Branch of the Saranac through one of the largest alder swamps in the Adirondacks. Like the other two waterways, the river offers an escape from motorboat traffic.

You can put in either at a bridge over the Rainbow Narrows or at the foot of Lake Kushaqua. By putting in at the bridge, you avoid a three-mile drive over rough road. You also avoid the powerboats that enter Kushaqua from a state boat launch on the east shore. If you want to see the lake, you can paddle down the Kushaqua Narrows from the bridge. This section is quite scenic. Another option is to start at the boat launch, which is part of the Buck Pond State Campground. There is a day-use fee when the campground is open (late May to early September).

The North Branch flows into the Rainbow Narrows just a tenth of a mile

The North Branch of the Saranac River. Photo by Susan Bibeau

west of the bridge. Turn north to enter the mouth, which has been widened by the dam at Kushaqua's outlet. Heading up the sluggish channel, you see stumps in the water where trees once stood on land. Ducks hang out in the weedy shallows, and turtles bask on logs. Hermit thrushes and white-throated sparrows call from the evergreen forest.

About a mile upriver, the current picks up briefly. You may need some elbow grease to reach a pool above the quick water. The pool offers a broad view over the alder swamp that lies ahead. Beyond here, the channel narrows as you meander through the shrubs and grasses. The shade of the alders keeps the water cool for brook trout.

Look for two fire towers as you venture deeper into the swamp: on Meenahga Mountain to the southwest and Loon Lake Mountain to the north. You can go about two miles up the North Branch before frequent beaver dams make travel impractical.

Upon returning to the Rainbow Narrows, turn right. Camps start to appear on the south shore, but most are fairly hidden. About a mile from the North Branch, you squeeze under a narrow bridge to enter Rainbow Lake proper.

You are now more likely to encounter motorboats, but you need to stay on the main lake for only a mile. Not long after entering the lake, you pass a wooded island. A larger island lies in the distance in the middle of the lake. When nearing this island, look to the lake's north shore for a narrow cut in the esker. After passing through the cut, you see a few camps on the east end of Clear Pond, but most of the shoreline is wild. Red pines grow on the slopes and crest of the esker. Paddle to the northwest corner of the pond to find a tiny canal with a concrete slab under the water. Legend has it that the gangster Legs Diamond once owned a camp in this spot and used the canal to escape police and other enemies. There is another cut near the southwest corner of Clear Pond.

Painted turtle Photo by Susan Bibeau

On the other side of the canal, bear right at the island dead ahead to enter the Flow. You won't find much flow in the Flow. The channel meanders through a sea of floating vegetation, past the spectral skeletons of drowned trees. As you go farther, the Flow gets narrower and the sense of remoteness grows. When you reach a large beaver dam, after a mile or so, it's time to turn around.

Upon returning to the island at the foot of the Flow, bear right. Presently, you enter a waterway known as the Inlet and begin to see camps on the esker. Paddle past the camps, keeping left of some boggy islands, to a wide cut in the esker. After going through the cut, take an immediate right to follow a narrow channel between the esker on the right and a marsh on the left. If you go part way down the channel and find your passage blocked by blowdown, look for an exit through the marsh. Otherwise, you can follow the channel for a half-mile. It leads to a little pool at the west end of Rainbow Lake. The takeout is on the right.

DIRECTIONS: From the intersection of Bloomingdale Avenue and Broadway in Saranac Lake, drive north on NY 86 for 8.3 miles to County 60 (Rainbow Lake Road) in the hamlet of Gabriels. Turn right and go 2 miles to County 31. Turn left and go 0.3 miles to Clark Wardner Road. Turn right and go 0.4 miles to a parking area on the left. There is a carry trail to Rainbow Lake across the road. This is the takeout. To reach the put-in, return to County 60 and turn left. Go 4.1 miles to Kushaqua-Mud Pond Road. Turn left and go 0.7 miles to the bridge over the Kushaqua Narrows. The GPS coordinates above are for this put-in. If want to continue to the foot of Lake Kushaqua, drive another 2.9 miles and put in on the far side of the bridge at the end of the lake.

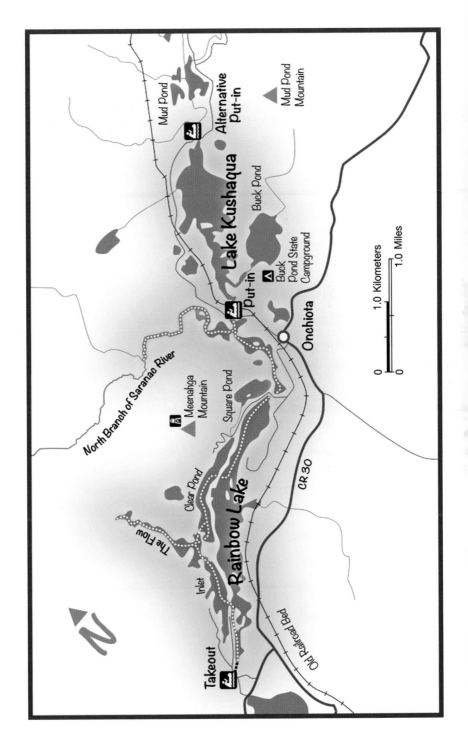

Mud Pond

Alternative
Put-in

Mud Pond
Mountain

Lake Kushaqua

Buck Pond

Buck
Pond State
Campground

Put-in

Onchiota

North Branch of Saranac River

Meenahga
Mountain

Square Pond

CR 30

Clear Pond

The Flow

Rainbow Lake

Inlet

Old Railroad Bed

Takeout

N

0   1.0 Kilometers
0   1.0 Miles

Confluence of Hatch Brook and Salmon River. Photo by Phil Brown

15. Hatch Brook & Salmon River

Length: 8 miles
Carries: None
Shuttle: 5 miles
Motors: Permitted
Put-in: 44°41.005' N, 74°11.461' W
Takeout: 44°44.195' N, 74°13.029' W
National Geographic map: Saranac/Paul Smiths

This cruise down Hatch Brook and the Salmon River proves that wildness and natural beauty exist outside the Blue Line. Although the trip begins in Porcaville, just inside the Adirondack Park, you spend most of your time winding through marshes and forestland north of the park boundary. Two state commissions, in 1970 and 1990, recommended that the park boundary be extended northward to include this stretch of the Salmon River, but the proposal evidently was deemed politically infeasible.

For the first mile from the put-in, Hatch Brook flows north through private land, passing several camps on the right bank, but the state owns the fishing rights along the left bank. The stream holds wild brook trout and is stocked with brown trout. At the start, you have to battle the alders on this narrow, twisting waterway. As you travel farther downstream, the alders become less of a nuisance.

Once you enter the Forest Preserve, the little stream is quite wild. Given the tightness of the channel, the views are limited to the alder thickets, grassy banks, treetops, clouds, and perhaps a trout rising for a fly. Look for wildlife tracks on the mudflats along the water's edge. You encounter a few beaver dams, but you should be able to get around or over them without leaving your boat. At 3.8 miles, you pass under a wooden snowmobile bridge and shortly thereafter reach the Salmon River.

The sandy confluence of the two streams—your halfway point—is a picturesque spot for a snack or swim. Adirondack paddlers might be struck by the flatness of the landscape here, with wild, green meadows stretching into the distance. The only prominent bump on the horizon is Owls Head Pinnacle to the north.

The Salmon River near the takeout. Photo by Phil Brown

The Salmon is wider than Hatch Brook and without the alder gantlets of its tributary. It's also less twisty, but you will find some sharp turns—most notably the Oxbow at 5.3 miles and the Needle's Eye at 6.2 miles, where the river's northward course is deflected by a steep hillside. Occasionally, you will be treated to views of the cliffs on Titusville Mountain to the west.

At 6.7 miles, you come to a quarter-mile straightaway at the end of which is a house on Studley Hill Road—a sign you are nearing the end of your trip. As you approach the house, the river turns right. This is known as The Bend. After making the turn, watch out for partially submerged boulders.

Less than a mile from the house is the takeout: a fishing-access site on the left bank. You could extend the trip three-quarters of a mile by paddling to the dam at Chasm Falls, but you've already seen the best scenery and the fishing-access site is a better takeout.

DIRECTIONS: From the junction of NY 30 and NY 86 in Paul Smiths, drive north on NY 30 for 17.5 miles to County 26. Turn right and drive 2.6 miles to Studley Hill Road. Turn left and go 6.2 miles to a DEC fishing-access site on the right. This is the takeout on the Salmon River. To reach the put-in, drive back on Studley Hill Road for 2.3 miles to a dirt road on the left (California Road). Turn and go 2.2 miles to another dirt road on the left (Run Road). Turn and drive 0.4 miles to its end at County 27. From here you can see a small bridge that crosses Hatch Brook. Put in at the bridge or at a bank along the road.

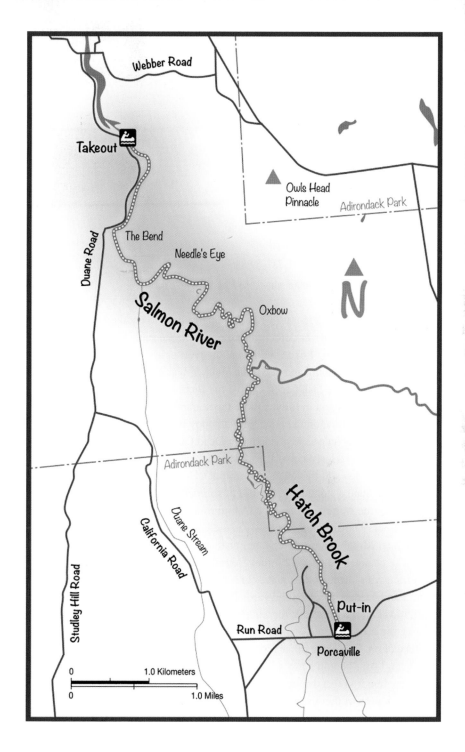

Webber Road

Takeout

Owls Head
Pinnacle

Adirondack Park

The Bend

Needle's Eye

N

Salmon River

Oxbow

Duane Road

Adirondack Park

Duane Stream

California Road

Hatch Brook

Studley Hill Road

Put-in

Run Road

Porcaville

0   1.0 Kilometers

0   1.0 Miles

16. Ausable Marsh

Length: 6.7 miles
Carries: 0.1 miles
Shuttle: None
Motors: Permitted
WSR status: Recreational
Put-in: 44°34.370' N, 73°25.988' W
National Geographic map: Lake Placid/High Peaks

Canoeists and kayakers rarely have an opportunity to paddle in a loop, but the Ausable River delta is an exception to the rule. About a mile and a half before reaching Lake Champlain, the river splits, allowing paddlers to travel up one channel and down the other. You could do this trip with no portage—unlike the Fish Creek Loop—but there is a variation with a short carry that enables you to fully explore the marsh between the two forks and minimizes your time on the potentially choppy waters of Lake Champlain.

The put-in is on a sandy beach near Dead Creek, a marsh that drains into the lake via a large culvert. Paddle southeast along the beach, taking in magnificent views of the lake and Vermont's Green Mountains. After a half-mile, you round a stone jetty; beware of submerged rocks here. Continue south past the Ausable Point State Campground and then head west toward the Ausable's north channel, known as the Upper Mouth. Instead of entering the Upper Mouth, go up the channel visible to its left.

The channel, reached 1.1 miles from the put-in, leads to a marsh teeming with birdlife and aquatic flora such as water lilies, pickerelweed, and pondweed. A few hundred yards from the lake, the channel splits. You can travel up the right fork for a quarter-mile before tufts of marsh grass block the way. En route you'll pass a beaver lodge. Returning to the watery intersection, follow the other fork for a half-mile. Just before reaching the end, land your boat in a low grassy section on the right, then drag or carry it a few hundred feet through the woods (there is no trail) to the bank on the Lower Mouth of the Ausable. The carry is short but mucky.

Once on the river, head upstream, passing under a railroad trestle and

Ausable Marsh in its fall colors. Photo by Carl Heilman II

Paddling Lake Champlain

At 435 square miles, Lake Champlain is the largest lake in the United States after the five Great Lakes. Champlain sees a lot of motorboat traffic and its waters are often whipped by the wind, so it's not ideal for paddling—especially in a canoe. For those who nonetheless want to venture onto the big lake, two trips are recommended.

Valcour Island. Put in at the boat launch on Route 9 in the town of Peru and paddle less than a mile to the lighthouse on Bluff Point. If you make a circuit of the island, taking in its coves, cliffs and beaches, the round-trip from the launch is about seven miles. Since Valcour is part of the Forest Preserve, you can land anywhere and hike the trail that traces the island's perimeter. There also are two crossover trails that cut through the interior of the island.

The Palisades. Put in at the boat launch on Route 9N in Westport and paddle northeast through the Champlain Narrows. On the New York side, cliffs known as the Palisades rise two hundred feet out of the water. Continue around Split Rock Point and take out at either the town beach at the west end of Whallon Bay or at Beggs Park in the hamlet of Essex. Depending your takeout, the one-way trip will be 10.5 or 13.3 miles.

Dead Creek Marsh near the put-in. Photo by Phil Brown

meandering past sandy banks. After a half-mile on the Lower Mouth, you come to the place where the main river divides. There is a large sandy beach near the fork, a good spot for a picnic or swim.

If you head upriver, you can go 0.6 miles to the Route 9 bridge. Rapids impede further progress. If you don't head upriver from the fork, you will immediately pass under another railroad trestle as you enter the river's Upper Mouth. You now have an easy downstream paddle of 1.5 miles through a lush bottomland forest dominated by silver maples. Then it's back on the lake to your starting point. The large sandbar near the mouth is another good place to swim.

Lake Champlain can get rough, so pick a calm day for this trip (or start at the Route 9 bridge to avoid the lake). If you do the circuit as described, you'll paddle 6.7 miles. You can extend it by taking the side trip to Route 9 or (even better) exploring Dead Creek Marsh, the habitat of mallards, geese, great blue herons, and other waterfowl.

DIRECTIONS: From Northway Exit 34, drive east on NY 9N for about a mile to its junction with NY 9 in the village of Keeseville. Turn left and go 6.2 miles to the entrance road for the Ausable Point State Campground (passing over the Ausable River en route). Turn right and go 0.7 miles to a parking area on the right next to the Dead Creek outlet. Put in at the beach across the road.

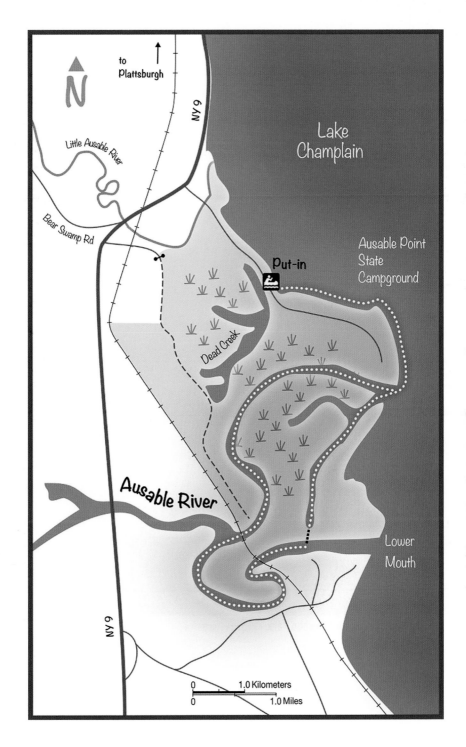

to
Plattsburgh

N

Little Ausable River

Bear Swamp Rd

NY 9

Lake
Champlain

Put-in

Ausable Point
State
Campground

Dead Creek

Ausable River

Lower
Mouth

NY 9

0   1.0 Kilometers
0   1.0 Miles

Lake Champlain at Noblewood Park. Photo by Phil Brown

17. Boquet River

Length: 4 miles round-trip
Carries: None
Shuttle: No
WSR status: Recreational
Motors: Permitted
Put-in: 44°22.058' N, 73°23.192' W
National Geographic map: Lake Placid/High Peaks

The Boquet River rises in the High Peaks, tumbling down mountains, rushing through gorges, and twisting through farmland on its way to Lake Champlain. Over the last few miles, the river is generally straight and calm, perfect for a novice paddler or a family outing.

This journey to Lake Champlain is one of the shortest trips in the book, so you should have plenty of time to loaf on the sandy spit at the river's mouth, play in the waves, and observe the waterfowl and other birds. Although it's generally an easy trip, be aware that after a heavy rain the current will be stronger.

The put-in ramp is just downstream from the river's last set of rapids. Landlocked salmon from Lake Champlain swim up the rapids to feed in spring and spawn in fall. After mounting a fish ladder in Willsboro, the fish may continue as far as Wadhams, some twelve miles from the lake. You can watch the salmon climb the fish ladder during their autumn runs.

Be careful when you put in as the river has a slight current near the ramp. At 0.65 miles from the

Spotted sandpiper Photo by Larry Master

Mouth of the Boquet River. Photo by Susan Bibeau

put-in, you come to a wooded island. At 1.5 miles, you can see Camel's Hump and other peaks in Vermont's Green Mountains. Soon after, the forest on the right shoreline gives way to a marsh. As you near the lake, beaches line both sides of the river. Keep paddling a little farther to the end of the sandy peninsula on the right bank.

The peninsula is part of Noblewood Park, one of the richest birding sites on Lake Champlain. Birders visit the park to look for a wide variety of waterbirds along the shore and on the lake, including sandpipers, plovers, herons, terns, and cormorants. They also seek out woodland birds on the forested trails.

Even if you're not a birder, you will enjoy lounging on the soft sand on a sunny afternoon and taking in the gorgeous views of the lake and the mountains of Vermont.

DIRECTIONS: From NY 22 in the hamlet of Willsboro, drive east on Gilliland Lane, which starts just south of the bridge over the Boquet and near the river's fish ladder. Go 0.5 miles to its end, passing en route an anglers' parking lot and a sewage plant. A ramp leads to the water.

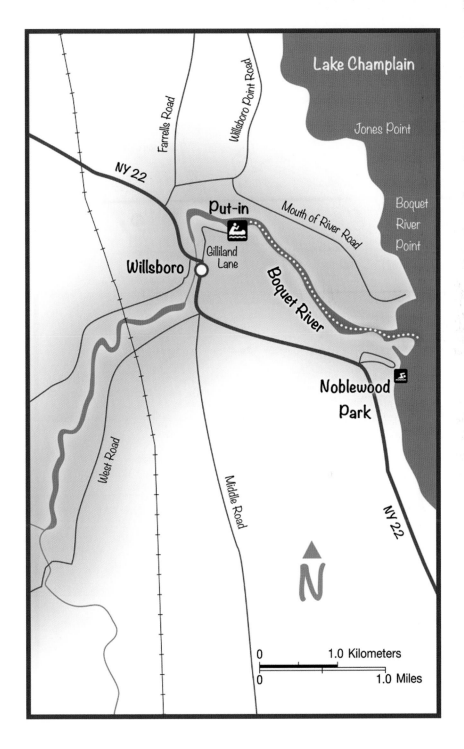

Lake Champlain

Jones Point

Farrells Road

Willsboro Point Road

NY 22

Put-in

Mouth of River Road

Boquet
River
Point

Gilliland
Lane

Willsboro

Boquet River

Noblewood
Park

West Road

Middle Road

NY 22

N

0   1.0 Kilometers

0   1.0 Miles

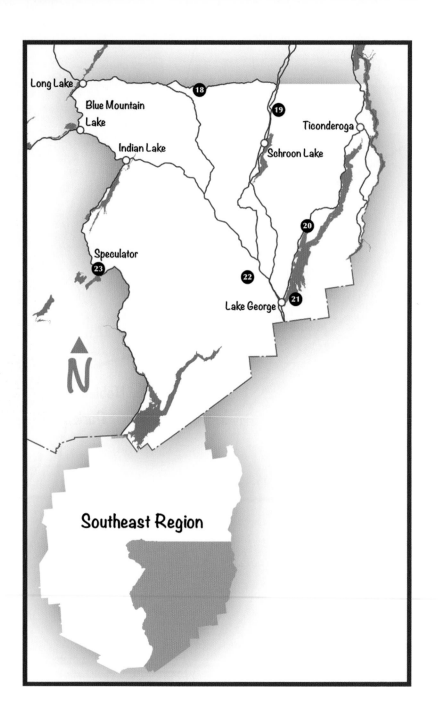

Long Lake

Blue Mountain
Lake

Indian Lake

18

19

Ticonderoga

Schroon Lake

20

Speculator

23

22

Lake George **21**

N

Southeast Region

The Kunjamuk River above Elm Lake. Photo by Phil Brown

SOUTHEAST REGION

18. Cheney Pond & Boreas River

Length: 6-7 miles round-trip
Carries: 0.5 miles if access road impassable
Shuttle: No
Motors: Permitted
Put-in: 43°56.440' N, 73°59.230' W
WSR status: Scenic
Meander quotient: 27%
National Geographic map: Lake Placid/High Peaks

In *Metamorphoses,* the Roman poet Ovid quotes an angry Boreas, the god of the North Wind: "By force I drive the weeping clouds, by force I whip the sea, send gnarled oaks crashing, pack the drifts of snow, and hurl the hailstones down upon the lands."

Not exactly great canoeing weather. And most of the Boreas River is not fit for canoeing, either. Like its namesake, the river is swift, violent, and vengeful. Though whitewater experts have paddled the rapids of the Boreas in optimal conditions, lesser mortals should keep away.

The one place where the Boreas relaxes is a two-and-a-half mile stretch above the ruins of an old logging dam in the Vanderwhacker Mountain Wild Forest. Old maps show this as a wide impoundment called Lester Flow, but the dam was breached long ago and the flow has since receded. Today, this part of the Boreas looks like a natural river.

Paddlers reach the Boreas by crossing Cheney Pond, named for the nineteenth-century guide John Cheney. If you have a high-clearance vehicle, you can drive to the pond's west shore on a rough dirt road. If not, you may have to carry or wheel your canoe a half-mile. From the put-in, paddle 0.6 miles straight across the pond, almost due east, to find the outlet. There's a large beach on the east shore with informal campsites and a lean-to that's set back from the water. Expect to see mergansers and other waterfowl on the pond.

The outlet is not always easy to discern. It begins as a shallow cut in the beach but soon deepens and reaches some rocks that obstruct passage. You can exit on the left bank and carry or drag your boat along a sandy path

A serene stretch of the Boreas River. Photo by Bob Kennedy

through the scrub. The outlet is just a quarter-mile long and the carry approximately 150 feet.

From where the outlet meets the river, you can paddle two miles downstream to the remains of the dam. The streamside scenery varies from alder swamp to bedrock outcrops to sandy banks topped by evergreens. The current also varies somewhat, but it's never so strong that you have to fret about the return trip. The river can be scratchy when water is low.

Although the Boreas has its share of turns, it's not as serpentine as many Adirondack rivers, such as the Oswegatchie or the North Branch of the Moose. It's also wider than many canoe streams: you won't be thrashing the alders on the way to Lester Dam. At the first bend, you come to a large boulder in the middle of the stream. You can get by it easily, but watch for shallows. A bit farther on, you pass a picnic table on the right bank—an odd sight in such a wild setting. If you plan to picnic, you may prefer to stop at one of the bedrock outcrops farther downstream.

After traveling 0.65 miles on the river, you come to an island: bear left to avoid a beaver dam to the right. Curling around the island, the river passes

The turnaround near Lester Dam. Photo by Justin Farrell

beneath a tall sand bank. After 1.4 miles, you paddle between two natural rock walls that extend several feet into the river. In another 0.4 miles you pass a grassy backwater on the right: look back to enjoy a view of the bare slabs on Gothics in the High Peaks Wilderness, some fifteen miles to the northeast.

The current picks up as the Boreas nears the remains of the dam, reached after 2.1 miles on the river (or 2.8 miles from your initial put-in). Pull out on the left and scramble up the bedrock for more views of Gothics and other peaks in the Great Range. Below the dam, the Boreas spills through rocky rapids for fifty yards before entering a quiet pool.

On the way back, you'll be treated to more mountain views. You can extend your trip by continuing upriver beyond the Cheney Pond outlet. It's possible to go nearly a half-mile before reaching rapids. After returning to the pond, you may want to try venturing up the pond's inlet, a narrow stream that winds through a grassy wetland on the southeast shore. Unless the water is high, though, you won't be able to get far.

DIRECTIONS: From Northway Exit 29, drive east on County 2 (Boreas Road) for 13.6 miles to a dirt road on the left, marked by a DEC sign for Cheney Pond; the turn is 1.9 miles west of the bridge over the Boreas River. If you're coming from the west, the turn is 4.3 miles east of the junction with Tahawus Road (County 25). The rough dirt road leads in 0.5 miles to Cheney Pond. It may be impassable to low-clearance vehicles.

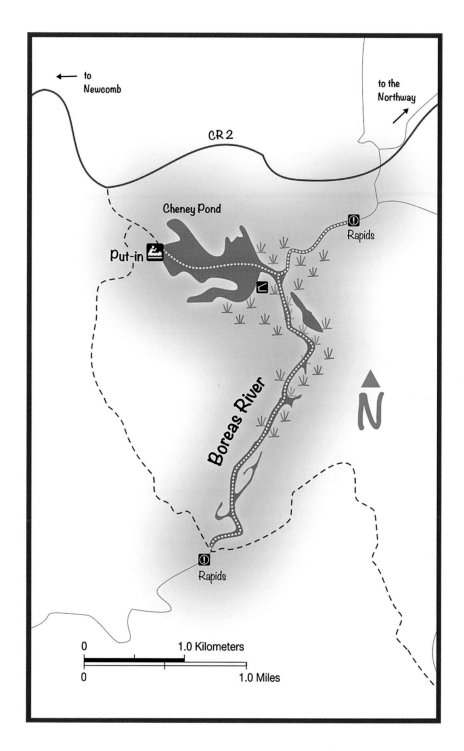

to
Newcomb

to the
Northway

CR 2

Cheney Pond

Rapids

Put-in

Boreas River

N

Rapids

0   1.0 Kilometers

0   1.0 Miles

19. Upper Schroon River

Length: Up to 12.5 miles
Carries: 0.1 miles
Shuttle: 4.6 miles
Motors: Permitted
WSR status: Recreational
Meander quotient: 54%
Put-in: 43°54.030' N, 73°44.875' W
Takeout: 43°50.131' N, 73°45.581' W
National Geographic map: Lake George/Great Sacandaga

The Schroon is one of the more accessible rivers in the Adirondacks, making it a favorite of anglers. The state has purchased fishing rights on lengthy stretches and stocks the river (or its lake) with brown trout, rainbow trout, brook trout, and salmon. If you like to fish while you paddle, a float trip on the Schroon may be just the ticket.

Even if you don't bring a pole, the Schroon has much to offer. North of Schroon Lake you can find miles and miles of meandering flatwater. In early spring, when water levels are high, you could put in at the Sharp Bridge State Campground and paddle some twenty miles to the lake (there are a few rapids). For most people, a more doable trip starts just downstream of Schroon Falls. From here, it's eight miles to the lake and another mile to the takeout in the hamlet of Schroon Lake. Shorter trips are also possible.

After leaving a second car or a bicycle in the hamlet, drive to a parking pull-off at the junction of Route 9 and River Road and then follow a short path through a stand of pines to rock ledges along the river. Take care when launching as the current below the falls is swift. Once on the water, ride out the current; it soon abates.

Rural roads border both sides of the river for much of the first few miles. Development is not intense, but you'll see a number of houses as well as an RV campground. Below Route 74, reached at 2.65 miles, the river gets wilder as it meanders through a broad floodplain forest. You could start the

The Schroon River in spring, with Hoffman Mountain in background. Photo by Phil Brown

trip here. If you do, park in a DEC lot just south of the highway bridge on the west side of the river.

Shortly after passing under Route 74, you come to the outlet of Paradox Lake on the left. When the Schroon floods in the spring, water in the outlet flows upstream, which accounts for the lake's name. When you reach the outlet, look back for the view of 3,693-foot Hoffman Mountain in the northwest. You have other views of Hoffman as the river twists through forest.

At 3.2 miles, the smaller but much closer Severance Hill rises in the west. This peak, too, will reappear from time to time. If you aren't tuckered out after the paddling trip, you can take a mile-long trail up Severance to a lookout with a view of Paradox Lake. (The trailhead is on the west side of Route 9.)

Although this stretch of the river is mostly wild, you will see two large houses on the right just before passing under Alder Meadow Road at 5.0

The marshes of Alder Creek. Photo by Phil Brown

miles. From this road to the lake, it's just over a mile as the crow flies but about three miles as the river flows. You can get in more turns by paddling up Alder Creek, which is reached about 1.5 miles below the bridge. It's possible to paddle in a short loop that begins at a fork reached just after you enter the creek. And if the water is high enough, you can go as far as 1.6 miles upstream to a culvert on Alder Meadow Road, where grassy wetlands offer more views of Hoffman Mountain and Severance Hill. If you make it that far, you'll need to contend with a few beaver dams en route.

Below Alder Creek, the Schroon winds through state-owned Forest Preserve, a great ending to your time on the river. Feel free to land on a beach for a swim or take a stroll through the lovely silver-maple forest. A mile below Alder Creek, or eight miles from Schroon Falls, you finally reach Schroon Lake. You still have nearly a mile to go. Paddle south across Lockwood Bay, round the point on the west shore, and take out at the town beach. When it's windy, the lake can by choppy. If you want to shorten your time on the lake, get permission beforehand to take out at the marina on Lockwood Bay.

DIRECTIONS: From Route 9 in downtown Schroon Lake, turn east onto Leland Avenue. Go 0.1 miles and turn right onto Dock Street. Go 0.1 miles to a boat-launch parking lot on the right. The lot is located across the road from the town beach (the takeout). For the put-in, return to Route 9 and drive north 4.5 miles to a small parking lot on the right at the junction with River Road. It is reached just after crossing the bridge at Schroon Falls. The path to the river starts on the other side of River Road.

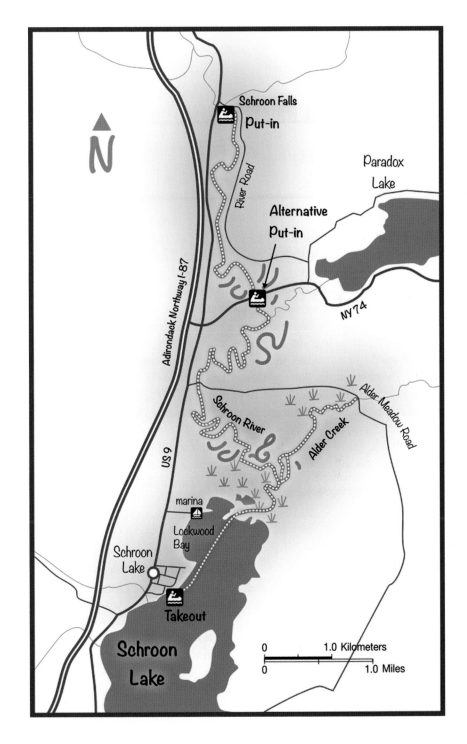

N

Schroon Falls
Put-in

Paradox
Lake

River Road

Alternative
Put-in

NY 74

Adirondack Northway I-87

Schroon River

Alder Creek

Alder Meadow Road

US 9

marina

Lockwood
Bay

Schroon
Lake

Takeout

Schroon
Lake

0   1.0 Kilometers

0   1.0 Miles

20. Northwest Bay Brook

Length: Up to 14 miles round-trip
Carries: None
Shuttle: No
Motors: Permitted
Put-in: 43°37.565' N, 73°36.440' W
National Geographic map: Lake George/Great Sacandaga

Lake George can be daunting to paddlers, especially those in open boats. If you're unsure about venturing onto the big lake, take a trip down the brook that leads to Northwest Bay. It's a worthwhile excursion in itself, and once you reach the bay, you can decide about paddling the lake.

If you do go on the lake, stay close to the bay's eastern shore. If you get as far as Montcalm Point, you can take a hike up the Tongue Mountain Range to First Peak or, better yet, to French Point Mountain for marvelous views of the lake. And if you paddle around Montcalm Point, you can explore the islands in the Narrows.

In the height of summer, the lake is often buzzing with powerboats and jet-skis, so this trip is best done in spring or after Labor Day.

Chestnut-sided warbler Photo by Larry Master

The start is at a state launch site for car-top craft. After putting in on Northwest Bay Brook, bear right and go around a bend. In 0.3 miles, you reach an opening on the left that leads to a marshy bay with a view of the Tongue Range. The bay has two lobes, and if you explore both to their ends, you'll get in more than a mile of paddling. Continuing down the brook, you reach Northwest Bay in another 0.8 miles. Thus, the distance from the put-in to the lake is only

Taking it easy on Northwest Bay Brook. Photo by Lori Van Buren

1.1 miles if you don't bother to explore the marsh on the way. With the side trip, the distance can be two miles or more.

Northwest Bay Brook is associated with one of the largest wetlands on Lake George. The wetland complex—which includes emergent marsh, wet meadows, alder scrub, and forested swamps—provides a rich environment for birdlife. The guidebook *Adirondack Birding* says a number of songbirds may be seen or heard in the brush at the start of the trip, such as blue-headed vireo, Baltimore oriole, chestnut-sided warbler, and American redstart. In the marsh are great-blue heron, least bittern, wood duck, mallard, and hooded and common merganser. Merlins nest in pines along the route.

Northwest Bay can be especially choppy when the wind blows from the south, so pick a calm day if you intend to continue your journey. A kayak is recommended over an open canoe. Three miles from the brook's mouth you come to Montcalm Point, the tip of the Tongue. The distinctive hump of Dome Island, a nature preserve, can be seen two miles to the south. Rounding Montcalm Point, you enter the Lake George Narrows, with dozens of islands of various sizes and shapes. Most of the islands are state-owned, and many are open to the public for camping for a fee. You can spend a few hours winding among the islands.

If you want to stretch your legs, land at Montcalm Point and pick up the

Looking down on Lake George from French Point Mountain. Photo by Lori Van Buren

Tongue Mountain hiking trail. It leads eleven miles over the spine of the range, traversing several summits and ending at Route 9N. You can obtain good views of the lake by climbing First Peak, whose summit is reached in 2.3 miles. Better views are found on French Point Mountain, reached in 3.7 miles. French Point's summit is more than 1,400 feet above the lake. Besides the lake and its islands, the vista includes Black Mountain, Buck Mountain, and numerous lesser peaks rising above the opposite shore. Timber rattlesnakes dwell on Tongue Mountain, but they are rarely seen by hikers.

If you explore the Narrows and the Northwest Bay Brook marshes and climb French Point Mountain, you'll have a full day: about fourteen miles of paddling and 6.4 miles of hiking. But the trip can be shortened to suit your schedule and ambitions. If you have only a few hours, they will be well spent in the scenic marshes.

DIRECTIONS: From Northway Exit 24, drive east on County 11 for 4.8 miles to a T-intersection with Route 9N. Turn left and go 4.4 miles to a parking lot on the right. For information about the Lake George Islands State Campground, visit the DEC website or call 518-457-2500.

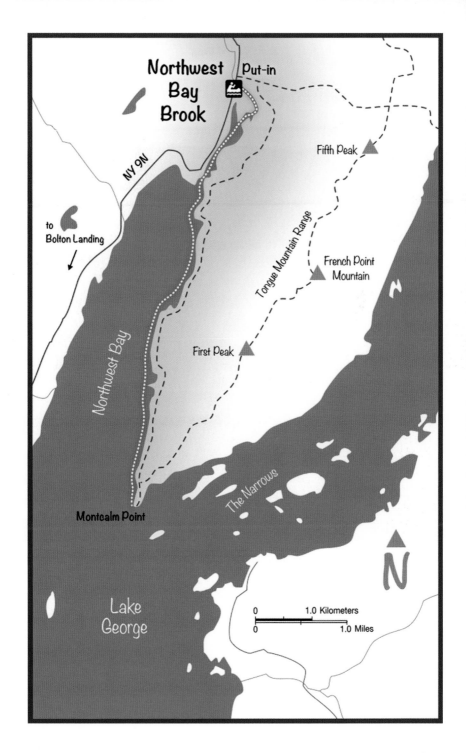

Northwest
Bay
Brook

Put-in

Fifth Peak

NY 9N

to
Bolton Landing

Tongue Mountain Range

French Point
Mountain

Northwest Bay

First Peak

The Narrows

Montcalm Point

N

Lake
George

0   1.0 Kilometers
0   1.0 Miles

Clouds and hills hovering over Dunham Bay Marsh.   Photo by Phil Brown

21. Dunham Bay Marsh

Length of trip: 4 miles round-trip
Carries: None
Shuttle: No
Motors: Permitted
Meander quotient: 29%
Put-in: 43°26.476' N, 73°39.267' W
National Geographic map: Lake George/Great Sacandaga

Lake George is the biggest and arguably the most beautiful lake inside the Adirondack Park, but with its winds and motorboat traffic, it is not everyone's ideal for paddling. Canoeists and kayakers can find a refuge from the busy lake in Dunham Bay Marsh.

The outlet of the vast marsh enters Lake George from the south. Starting at Dunham's Bay Marina, you can travel two miles up the channel. The marina charges paddlers a small fee ($5 per boat in 2012) for launch privileges.

The trip begins at a grassy area near some boat slips. The stream seems to have no current. In truth, it is not a stream at all but an extension of the lake. Writing in the *Adirondack Explorer* newsmagazine, the photographer Mark Bowie likens it to an ocean estuary. "This marsh's ocean is Lake George," he says, "and it's dependent upon the lake for its ebb and flow."

Though boxed in by roads, the marsh is a natural oasis that abounds in fish, fowl, and other wildlife. As you head deeper into the wetland, you're likely to flush great blue herons, ducks, and geese. Red-winged blackbirds frequently flit across the water and call out from the cattails. You'll also see a few beaver lodges. Water lilies and pickerelweed flourish in the calm water.

The scenery changes with every bend in the stream. Perhaps the best view is to the northeast, looking over the marsh grasses toward Pilot's Knob and the rocky summit of Buck Mountain. Sugarloaf Mountain is closer and directly east.

At 1.5 miles, the stream becomes weedier and soon becomes clogged

Meandering in the marsh. Photo by Phil Brown

with lily pads as well. If you push on, the lily pads thin out, though the weeds remain. At about two miles, you reach the channel's end in a hard-wood forest. In summer, you may find the place abuzz with cedar waxwings.

On the way back, you'll often have the rocky ledges of Cat Mountain in your sights. The peak is located in the northwest, about halfway up the lake.

DIRECTIONS: From Northway Exit 21, drive east for 0.1 miles to a T-intersection. Turn left onto NY 9 and go 0.3 miles to NY 9L. Turn right and go 4.6 miles to Bay Road. Turn right and then make a quick left into the marina parking lot to pay your parking fee. Afterward, continue another 0.2 miles down Bay Road to the access road for the put-in.

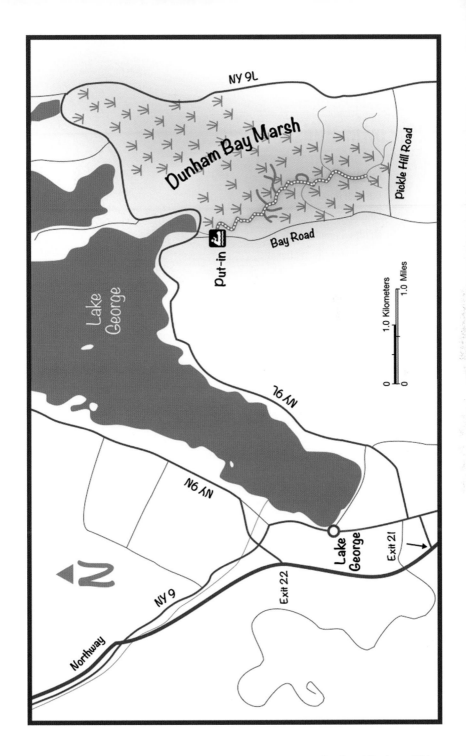

22. Lower Hudson River

Length: 13 miles
Carries: None
Shuttle: About 18 miles
Motors: Permitted
WSR status: Recreational
Meander quotient: 14%
Put-in: 43°28.818' N, 73°49.151' W
Takeout: 43°19.538' N, 73°51.209' W
National Geographic map: Lake George/Great Sacandaga

Among whitewater enthusiasts, the Hudson River has a wild reputation, and anyone who has paddled or rafted through the Hudson Gorge knows it's well deserved. But as it approaches the southern border of the Adirondack Park, the river shows its mellow side. The best way to experience the laid-back Hudson is on a thirteen-mile downstream cruise from Thurman Station south of Warrensburg to a takeout north of Lake Luzerne village.

Most of the land along the route is private, with some development on the west bank, but you also pass through the state-owned Hudson River Recreation Area, where you can stop for lunch or a swim. In fact, for a shorter trip (less than eight miles) and easier shuttle, you can put in at the north end of the HRRA.

At Thurman Station, you put in near the bridge that carries Route 418 over the river. Soon after entering the water, you experience the strongest current on the whole trip. This is only the first of several riffles you'll encounter throughout the day. If the water is shallow, you may scrape bottom in some of them, and in a few places, you may even need to walk your boat. Most of the time, though, the current is your friend.

In a few miles, you come to first of many islands on this excursion. They are all undeveloped, but most are privately owned. Look for ducks and mergansers in the side channels and along the grassy shorelines.

White pines along the Hudson River. Photo by Ray Palmer

You won't see big mountains on this stretch of the Hudson, but the local hills often rise steeply above the river, some with rocky cliffs. Drifting with the current, admiring the scenery, looking up at the clouds—at times it's idyllic. At other times, though, the spell of nature is broken by a passing car or, for example, the appearance of a dude ranch.

After five and a half miles, you reach the Hudson River Recreation Area, a long strip of Forest Preserve on the east bank with a number of car-camping sites. On a nice summer day, especially on weekends, you'll see people swimming, paddling, fishing, floating on inner tubes, or just hanging out. You'll also pass two canoe launches in quick succession, one with a wheelchair ramp, the other with wooden steps. Either of these can be used as a put-in for a shorter version of this trip. A bit farther on, about six miles from Thurman Station, Stony Creek flows into the Hudson from the west.

Tubers in the Hudson River Recreation Area. Photo by Phil Brown

After leaving the Hudson River Recreation Area, you see fields and more homes and camps. Be sure not to miss the takeout, for dangerous falls lie less than a mile ahead in the village of Lake Luzerne. The takeout is marked by a brown-and-yellow "Canoe Access" sign.

DIRECTIONS: From the junction of Main and Bridge streets in the village of Lake Luzerne, drive north on Main to Mill Street. Turn left and go 0.8 miles to a parking area on the right. The takeout is on the opposite side of the road. If opting for the shorter trip, continue driving north 7.8 miles (much of it on dirt road) to a turnaround and look for the put-in on the left. If starting at Thurman Station, return to Bridge Street, turn right, and go 0.4 miles (crossing the Hudson) to County 1. Turn right, heading toward the hamlet of Stony Creek, and go 8.1 miles to Grist Mill Road. Turn right and go 0.2 miles to a T-intersection. Turn right and go 8.1 miles to the Thurman Station depot. Turn right and go 0.2 miles to a parking area near the river.

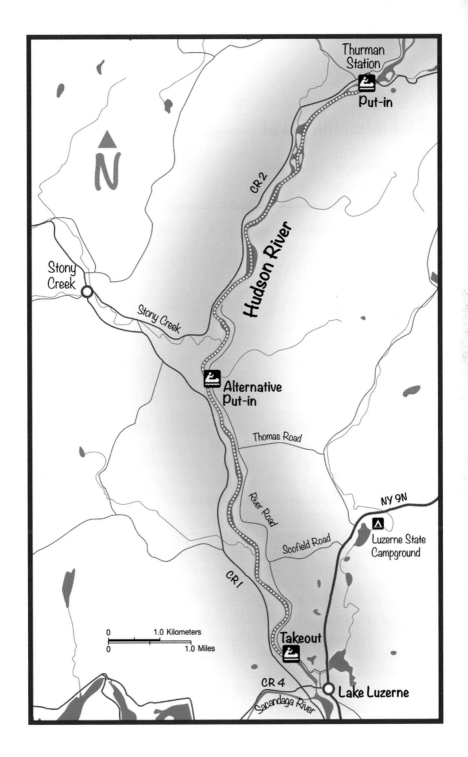

23. Kunjamuk River

Length: 13 miles round-trip
Carries: None
Shuttle: No
WSR status: Scenic
Motors: Permitted
Meander quotient: 35%
Put-in: 43°29.744' N, 74°21.525' W
National Geographic map: Northville/Raquette Lake

Paddling small streams is a delightful way to experience the wild, but the views are often limited by the closeness of the forest or alder thickets. So it is with the Kunjamuk River until you reach Elm Lake, where a broad mountain vista unfolds beyond a vast marsh. On a sunny day with a few puffy clouds on the horizon the scenery is about as good as it gets.

To get the most out of the trip, start in the village of Speculator. Put in at a boat launch on the Sacandaga River and paddle downstream for 1.6 miles to Kunjamuk Bay, where the two rivers join forces. For a shorter trip, you could put in at Kunjamuk Bay from Route 30 south of Speculator, but you'd miss out on a delightful stretch of the Sacandaga.

The Sacandaga channel is narrow at the outset, full of pickerelweed, water lilies, and friendly ducks, but it soon broadens to offer views of nearby Oak Mountain, Cave Hill, and Rift Hill as well as more distant peaks. After a half-mile, you'll notice a dock on the left. If you feel like a walk on the way back, you can leave your boat here and follow a nature trail known as the Sacandaga Pathway.

Beyond the dock, the river meanders through an expansive marsh that teems with herons, ducks, and other birdlife. As you enter Kunjamuk Bay, Speculator Mountain is due south. Turn left and paddle a few hundred feet to find the mouth of the Kunjamuk.

Heading upriver, you encounter several beaver dams, but most of these have been breached in recent years. If you're lucky, you'll have to get out of

Approaching Elm Lake on the Kunjamuk River. Photo by Phil Brown

your canoe only once or twice on the way to Elm Lake.

The land bordering the Kunjamuk is owned by a timber company, but you won't see evidence of logging from the water. The habitat along the twisty stream varies from marsh to alders to hardwood forest. In mid-summer, you'll see a lot of cardinal flowers, turtlehead, Joe-Pye weed, buttonbush, pickerelweed, and pond lilies in bloom.

About 1.8 miles from the mouth, you come to the first of two logging-road bridges. The mysterious Kunjamuk Cave, a local curiosity, can be found just a quarter-mile up the road. No one knows for sure who created the small cave or why. A hole in the roof lets in sunlight. To visit the cave, land your canoe at a small muddy strand on the left just beyond the bridge. Cross the bridge and head east along the road to a signpost on the left. The cave lies just a hundred feet off the road at the end of a well-worn path.

Continuing the journey upstream, you pass under the second bridge in another mile or so. Soon after, you start to see views of Dug Mountain and East Mountain. The river widens as you wind through fields of pickerelweed before entering Elm Lake, about 3.7 miles from Kunjamuk Bay.

Visiting a beaver lodge above Elm Lake. Photo by Phil Brown

Except for three small camps on the east shore, the lake is wild. A large marsh on the far end affords fantastic views not only of Dug and East, but also of more distant peaks, including Upper Pine Mountain and Mossy Mountain.

For the best scenery, paddle to the head of the lake and pick up the river again. You'll soon reach a large beaver dam, but it's worth carrying over to see a little more of the Kunjamuk. The second impassable beaver dam is about a half-mile from the lake—a good spot to turn around. Those not put off by frequent dams can push on deeper into the marsh.

If you start in Speculator, the round trip is thirteen miles. If you launch in Kunjamuk Bay, the trip will be ten miles.

DIRECTIONS: From the intersection of NY 8 and NY 30 in Speculator, drive south on NY 8/30 for 0.5 miles to a large parking lot on the left, reached just before the road crosses the river. If you want to put in at Kunjamuk Bay, continue south for another 1.4 miles to a pull-off on the left (43°30.042' N, 74°20.164' W).

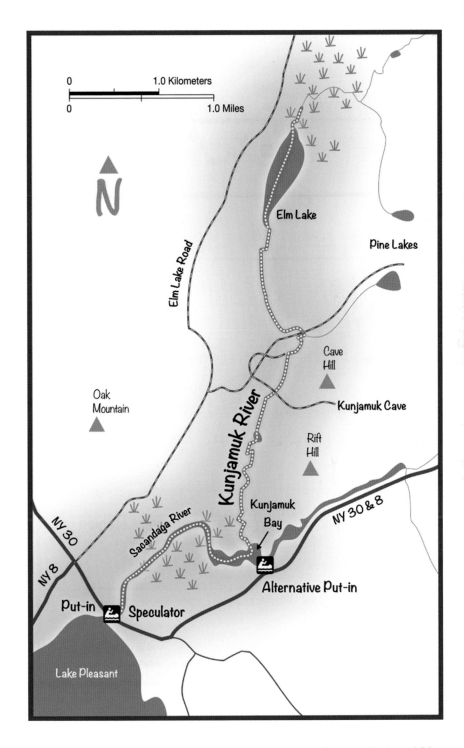

0
1.0 Kilometers

0
1.0 Miles

N

Elm Lake Road

Elm Lake

Pine Lakes

Oak Mountain

Cave Hill

Kunjamuk Cave

Kunjamuk River

Rift Hill

Sacandaga River

Kunjamuk Bay

NY 30

NY 8

NY 30 & 8

Alternative Put-in

Put-in   Speculator

Lake Pleasant

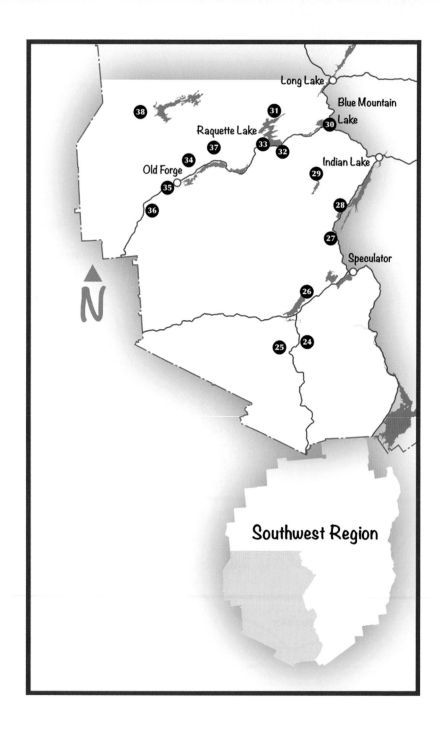

Long Lake

Blue Mountain Lake

38

31

Raquette Lake

37   33 32

34   Indian Lake

Old Forge

35   29

36   28

27

Speculator

N

26

25   24

Southwest Region

Fall Stream. Photo by Mark Bowie

SOUTHWEST REGION

24. West Branch of Sacandaga

Length: up to 9.5 miles
Carries: None
Shuttle: 6 miles
Motors: Prohibited
WSR status: Wild
Meander quotient: 41%
Put-in: 43°15.328' N, 74°32.1512' W
Takeout: 43°19.453' N, 74°32.205' W
National Geographic map: Northville/Raquette Lake

The name *Sacandaga* is said to derive from a Native American word meaning either "land of waving grass" or "drowned land." Paddlers will find justification for both interpretations on this lazy stretch of the West Branch. Meandering downriver, you do see waving grass, both in the broad meadows and in the gentle current. But if you step out of your boat and sink up to your knee in muck, you might conclude that *drowned* is a more fitting epithet, along with a few others.

If the semantics are muddy, the beauty of the West Branch of the Sacandaga is obvious to all who have paddled it. Barbara McMartin, a prolific author of guidebooks, once wrote: "The river has everything: remoteness, surrounding small mountains, meanders through marshes and fields of flowers and butterflies."

The best way to see the West Branch is on a through trip from a bridge on Route 10 to a takeout down the road. It's an eight-mile paddle between endpoints, but it'd be a shame to miss three ponds along the way: Chub Lake, Trout Lake, and Little Trout Lake. These detours will add 1.5 miles to the trip.

From the takeout near Shaker Place Road, it's an easy six-mile bike ride or drive back to the put-in. If you want to avoid a shuttle, you can paddle to the ponds and back—about eight miles round-trip. In either case, you can extend the trip by paddling upriver from the start to Good Luck Lake.

For most of the route the river flows through sedge meadows and alder

A peaceful day on the West Branch of the Sacandaga. Photo by Mark Bowie

thickets. The low vegetation allows paddlers to enjoy views of nearby hills throughout the trip. For scenery close at hand, look for blooms of Joe-Pye weed, swamp azalea, cardinal flower, buttonbush, and purple-stem angelica, among others. You also may see ducks, mergansers, herons, and red-winged blackbirds and perhaps a beaver or an otter.

From the put-in, head downstream and start searching the right bank for the Chub Lake outlet, reached in a quarter-mile. A narrow channel leads in 0.2 miles to the seventeen-acre pond. Leatherleaf, pitcher plants, bog rosemary, rose pogonia, and other bog vegetation line the shores of the outlet and the pond. Cranberries appear in late summer.

Below the Chub Lake outlet, the river winds between the highway and Trout Lake Mountain. As you pass the mountain, look for Trout Lake to the east. At 2.2 miles from the put-in (not including the detour to Chub Lake), you reach the short outlet. Nick Stoner, a Revolutionary soldier and legendary woodsman, sometimes stayed in a bark shanty near the outlet while trapping beaver on the West Branch. Usually, the water is high enough to paddle to Trout and Little Trout lakes. Go to the north end of Trout Lake to find the channel to its smaller neighbor. The round-trip from the river to Little Trout is about a mile.

Heading for the hills. Photo by Mark Bowie

Just beyond Trout Lake, the West Branch pulls close to the road and passes several buildings on private land. It generally parallels the road, alternately turning toward and away from it, for the next two miles until reaching Averys Place, once the site of a popular hotel. There, the river bumps against Pine Mountain and turns east.

Soon after turning north again, the West Branch is joined by the outlet of Loomis Pond and then bends northwest as it skirts the other side of Pine Mountain. At 7.4 miles, after more meandering through grassy meadows, the river comes close to the highway again. The state plans to build a waterway-access site along Shaker Place Road, but until then you must take out along Route 10 and scramble up the bank. So be sure to exit the river before it pulls away from the highway for good.

DIRECTIONS: From Caroga Lake, drive north on NY 10 to the second bridge over the West Branch, reached 2.9 miles after crossing the Hamilton County line. The parking area is on the right on the north side of the bridge. To reach the takeout, drive 6.4 miles north to Shaker Place Road on the right. Until the state builds an access facility on Shaker Place Road, the actual takeout will be on NY 10 a bit south of Shaker Place Road.

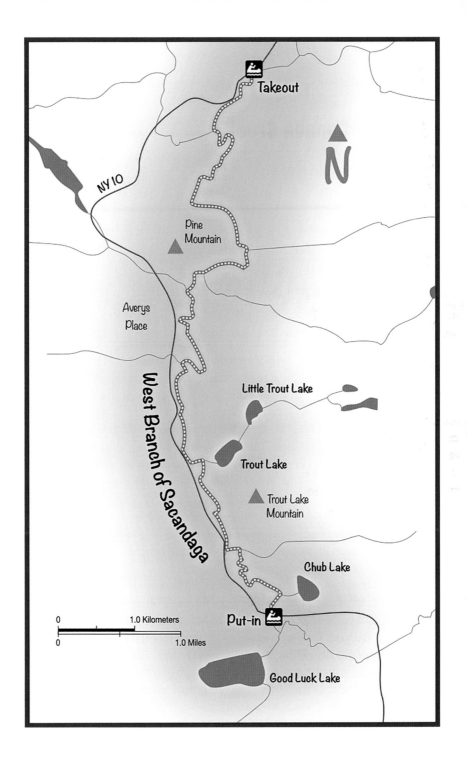

Takeout

N

NY 10

Pine
Mountain

Averys
Place

West Branch of Sacandaga

Little Trout Lake

Trout Lake

Trout Lake
Mountain

Chub Lake

0   1.0 Kilometers
0   1.0 Miles

Put-in

Good Luck Lake

25. East Canada Creek

Length: 4 miles round-trip
Carries: None
Shuttle: No
Motors: Permitted
WSR status: Scenic
Put-in: 43°18.591', 74°39.262' W
National Geographic map: Northville/Raquette Lake

East Canada Creek has a reputation as a whitewater boater's stream, but flatwater paddlers can enjoy a meandering stretch near its headwaters. Although the trip is short, that leaves time to take in the many other attractions along Powley-Piseco Road, a dirt thoroughfare that passes through old-growth forest.

The put-in is at Powley Place, a clearing near one of the largest wetlands in the Ferris Lake Wild Forest. The clearing is well known to birders. Gary Lee, one of the authors of *Adirondack Birding,* once saw the rare American three-toed woodpecker here. Another boreal bird, the olive-sided flycatcher, also can be found.

From the iron bridge at Powley Place, you can paddle almost two miles downstream before reaching rapids. First, however, try paddling upstream. The way will soon be blocked by beaver dams and/or alders, but it's fun to see how far you can go.

After turning around and passing under the bridge, look for a grassy inlet on the left about a quarter-mile from the road. Go up the inlet into a marsh to take in the view of Big Alderbed Mountain to the west.

Below the inlet, the East Canada winds south through marshes and alder thickets, occasionally pulling beside the mossy forest. The stream corridor parallels Sugarbush Mountain, which rises nearby on the right. Depending on the time of year, you may see along the creek blooms of mountain ash, wild raisin, mountain laurel, or gentian.

East Canada Creek. Photo by Nancy L. Ford

The put-in bridge on Powley-Piseco Road. Photo by Nancy L. Ford

A mile from the bridge, you come to a long straightaway and a low beaver dam that usually can be paddled over with no problem. A half-mile farther on, after rounding a bend, you start to hear whitewater. Soon the stream splits in two as it flows around an island at the head of the rapids. You can find refuge in a marshy pool on the right. This is the place to turn around. In the cascades below, the East Canada drops fifteen feet.

On the return, you'll be treated to numerous views of the peaks to the north. Although you'll be heading upstream, the current is seldom noticeable. You can relax and enjoy the scenery and the birdsong.

In all, you can get in about four miles of flatwater paddling. Afterward, you may want to visit the Potholers, a delightful picnic spot near the confluence of the East Canada and Brayhouse Brook. The East Canada has eroded large holes in the flat bedrock, some large enough to sit in. To reach the Potholers, drive 2.7 miles south from Powley Place and look for a short path on the left that starts near a culvert.

Several unmarked hiking trails also start along Powley-Piseco Road. One of the best leads to cascades on Goldmine Stream. For details on the hiking possibilities, consult ADK's *Adirondack Trails: Southern Region.*

Finally, if you want to do more paddling, check out Big Bay, a 2.5-mile-long impoundment on Piseco Outlet. The put-in for Big Bay is on State Route 10, just a tenth of a mile north of the northern end of Powley-Piseco Road.

DIRECTIONS: From the junction of NY 8 and NY 30 in Speculator, drive west on NY 8 for 12.4 miles to NY 10. Turn left and go 1.2 miles to Powley-Piseco Road. Turn right and go 8.2 miles to an iron bridge over East Canada Creek. Put in near the southwest corner of the bridge.

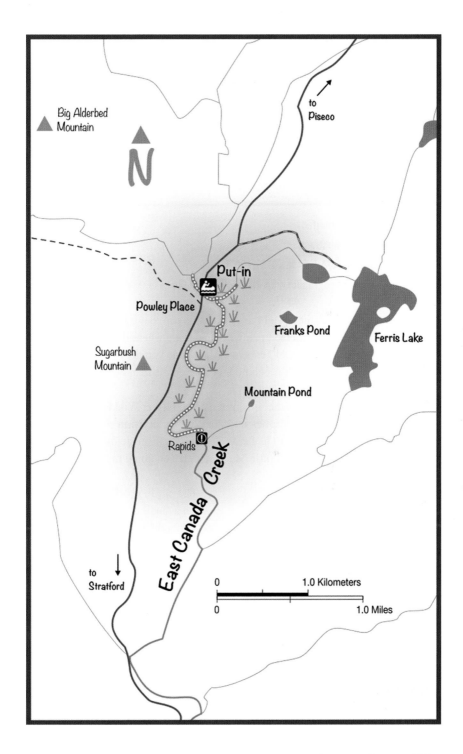

26. Fall Stream

Length: Up to 11 miles round-trip
Carries: None
Shuttle: No
Motors: Permitted
Meander quotient: 33%
Put-in: 43°26.592' N, 74°31.109' W
National Geographic map: Northville/Raquette Lake.

You might see a few camps at the start of this trip, but it's not long before you find yourself immersed in a wild landscape where the only edifices are the dams and domiciles of beavers. By the time you get to Vly Lake, you'll have left civilization far behind and entered the marshy realm of great blue herons and red-winged blackbirds.

Fall Stream flows out of the hills of the Jessup River Wild Forest in the southern Adirondacks and empties into Piseco Lake. Even in summer you usually can follow Fall Stream as far as Vly Lake, a distance of five miles, and some paddlers push on to little Mud Lake. If you go all the way to Mud, be ready to get your feet wet.

Pickerelweed   Photo by Phil Brown

The put-in is off Old Piseco Road, at a small dock just a stone's throw from the mouth and just upstream of some shallow rapids. At the start of the trip, you are paddling through private property, so do not land or otherwise violate the landowners' rights.

The stream is broad and placid as it meanders lazily past alder thickets and patches of pickerelweed. Expect to see lots of pickerelweed on this trip. The plant grows in shallow water, its roots anchored

Fall Stream. Photo by Mark Bowie

deep in muck; in midsummer its flowered spikes turn a vibrant purple. As you travel upstream, look for blooms of cardinal flowers and turtleheads on the water's edge—as well as otter, deer, and muskrat tracks.

Not long into the trip, you round a bend and catch sight of Oxbow Mountain in the east. After about a mile, you come to a dock and a side channel that leads to a private camp. Just beyond the dock, you enter the Forest Preserve. The stream broadens as it morphs into Fall Lake, reached at 1.5 miles. This twenty-four-acre lake contains several species of fish, including chain pickerel, brown bullhead, and smallmouth bass.

Paddle up the lake toward a large colony of pickerelweed and keep left of the plants to find the inlet. Fall Stream now becomes shallower, more meandering, more intimate. Grassy banks yield for a while to forest, with trees overhanging the water. On the way to Vly, you encounter several beaver dams. If water levels are high, you should be able to paddle over most of them—or through them, thanks to breaches—but you likely will have to exit your boat a few times. If the water is low, you'll have a harder time.

Just past one big dam, nearly four miles from the put-in, you snake

Dropping over a beaver dam. Photo by Phil Brown

through a zone of dead alders and then follow a straightaway that leads to Vly. True to its name (in Dutch, *vly* refers to a swampy area), most of the shoreline of this small, wild lake is boggy, but if you paddle up the right shore you'll find rock outcrops where you can camp or picnic.

Hidden in the weeds on the opposite side of the lake is the Mud Lake outlet. This tiny stream is muddy, shallow, and obstructed by beaver dams, but those who don't mind a little adventure can follow it for four-tenths of a mile to the lake. If you need to step out of your boat to pull over a dam, be prepared to sink into muck.

Most people probably will be content to turn around at Vly, making a round trip of about ten miles. This gives them more time to appreciate the serenity and scenery (including a fine view of Vly Lake Mountain) found on this pearl of a lake.

Despite all the beaver dams on Fall Stream, anglers sometimes take small outboards to Vly Lake to catch pike and other fish. They probably helped create the breaches in the dams. If so, you'll have the fishermen to thank if you manage to get back to your starting point without exiting your canoe or kayak.

DIRECTIONS: From the four corners in Speculator, turn west onto NY 8 and drive 9.0 miles to Old Piseco Road (County 24). Turn right and go 1.6 miles to the bridge over Fall Stream. Look for a short path on the right after crossing the bridge.

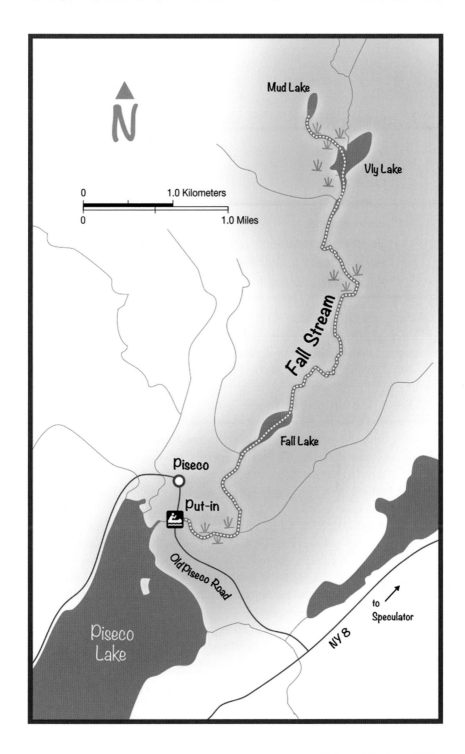

27. Jessup River

Length: 8 miles round-trip
Carries: None
Shuttle: No
Motors: Permitted
Meander quotient: 51%
Put-in: 43°34.961' N, 74°24.393' W
National Geographic map: Northville/Raquette Lake

After putting in the Jessup River from Route 30, you have a decision to make: should you go downstream toward Indian Lake or upstream through a seldom-visited tract of Forest Preserve? The answer: both.

But if you had to choose one over the other, the upstream trip has a wilder feel. From the put-in you usually can paddle at least three miles up the Jessup. The current offers little resistance, but you likely will have to carry around some beaver dams and blowdown.

The trout stream winds through alders and marsh much of the way, but it does pull alongside the forest in places, offering welcome shade on a hot day. In summer, you can see blooms of Joe-Pye weed, cardinal flower, and red osier. The sandy flats on the bends are ideal places to stop for a swim or picnic.

If you push on, you might be able to make it all the way to Jessup River Road, a dirt road that runs through forestland owned by a timber company. If the river is high enough, this road could serve as an alternative put-in for a one-way downstream paddle of about four miles to Route 30. (The state owns a public easement on the timberlands. If you choose to put-in here, do not block the road with your car.)

When you've gone upstream as far as you want, return to Route 30 but pass under the highway and keep paddling. You'll enjoy more flatwater as the river continues to wind past alder swamps and woodlands. Chances are you'll have to scoot over a beaver dam or two.

A little over a mile from the highway, you come to a cable stretched across the river, signaling the start of a long stretch of moderate rapids. If

Unwinding on the Jessup River above the Route 30 put-in. Photo by Phil Brown

Dug Mountain Brook Falls. Photo by Mark Bowie

you have a sturdy boat and whitewater experience, you can run the rapids in high water. It's also possible to portage a half-mile on a rough path along the right bank. Once beyond the rapids, you could follow the Jessup to a narrow arm of Indian Lake and eventually take out at the Indian Lake Islands State Campground (day-use fee required) or at the Route 30 bridge over the Miami River.

If you do paddle to Indian Lake, be sure to check out Dug Mountain Brook Falls. Dug Mountain Brook enters the Jessup a quarter-mile beyond the rapids. Land on the north side of the brook and follow an unmarked path about a quarter-mile to the falls. If you plan to paddle only as far as the rapids you can still visit the waterfall. Simply follow the carry path to Dug Mountain Brook and then pick up the other trail. The two-mile hike (round-trip) is a fine way to cap a day of paddling.

DIRECTIONS: From the intersection of NY 8 and NY 30 in Speculator, drive north on NY 30 for 6.5 miles to the bridge over the Jessup. There are pull-offs on the north side of the bridge on both sides of the highway. Also, a short but rough road south of the bridge leads from the west side of the highway to a third put-in. If coming from the north, the river is reached 17.5 miles from the junction of NY 30 and NY 28 in Indian Lake.

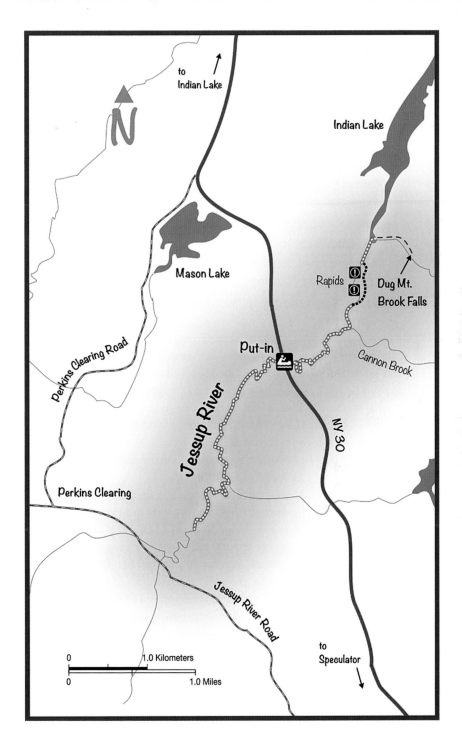

to
Indian Lake

N

Indian Lake

Mason Lake

Perkins Clearing Road

Rapids

Dug Mt.
Brook Falls

Put-in

Cannon Brook

Jessup River

NY 30

Perkins Clearing

0   1.0 Kilometers

0   1.0 Miles

Jessup River Road

to
Speculator

28. Miami River

Length: 9 miles round-trip
Carries: None
Shuttle: No
Motors: Permitted
WSR status: Study River
Meander quotient: 50%
Put-in: 43°39.092' N, 74°23.389' W
National Geographic map: Northville/Raquette Lake

The early settlers of these cold mountains must have harbored secret yearnings for warmer climes. How else to explain such toponyms as Pharaoh Mountain? Mount Arab? Or the Miami River? If you set out for the Miami from Lewey Lake, you'll be headed in the right direction: south. You won't get all the way to Florida, but you may see some fine beaches.

You can start at the Lewey Lake State Campground, but you'll have to pay a day-use fee if it's open. To avoid the fee, park along Route 30 near the bridge over the Miami north of the campground's main entrance. Put in the north side of the river just upstream of the bridge.

Paddling upriver, you pass several tent sites. The abundance of mallards in the sluggish channel in summer leads to a suspicion that they're mooching crumbs from the campers. In a half-mile, you reach Lewey Lake, once the haunt of the hermit French Louie. From the lake you enjoy impressive views of some of the highest Adirondack summits outside the High Peaks region, including Lewey and Snowy mountains.

To pick up the Miami again, paddle to the south end of the lake, aiming for a notch in the hills. More than a mile long, Lewey Lake is surrounded largely by Forest Preserve, but there are a private a cabin and a small resort on the east shore.

After paddling 1.85 miles from the put-in, you reach the end of the lake. The river is partially hidden in the pickerelweed and marsh grasses, but once you find it, there's no mistaking it. At the start, the low vegetation along

View of Snowy Mountain from the Miami River. Photo by Mark Bowie

A misty morning on the Miami.   Photo by Mark Bowie

the banks allows for fairly open views of the nearby hills. As you progress upriver, the views become more constricted by alders and woods.

A half-mile from the lake, you come to a large beaver dam and, soon after, the first of several lodges. You'll encounter a number of other dams as well; chances are you'll be able to paddle over most—or through them if they've been breached by other canoeists.

The Miami has a lot of twists and turns, and sometimes you end up going down a cul-de-sac, but that's all part of the fun. You can paddle about two and a half miles from the lake without much trouble and farther if you don't mind pulling over dams. How far? Who knows, maybe to Florida. But then you'd miss the great views of the mountains on the return across Lewey Lake.

DIRECTIONS: From the intersection of NY 8 and NY 30 in Speculator, drive north on NY 30 for 12.4 miles to the bridge over the Miami. There is room to park off the road's shoulder. If you're coming from the north, you reach the bridge in 11.9 miles from the junction of NY 30 and NY 28 in Indian Lake.

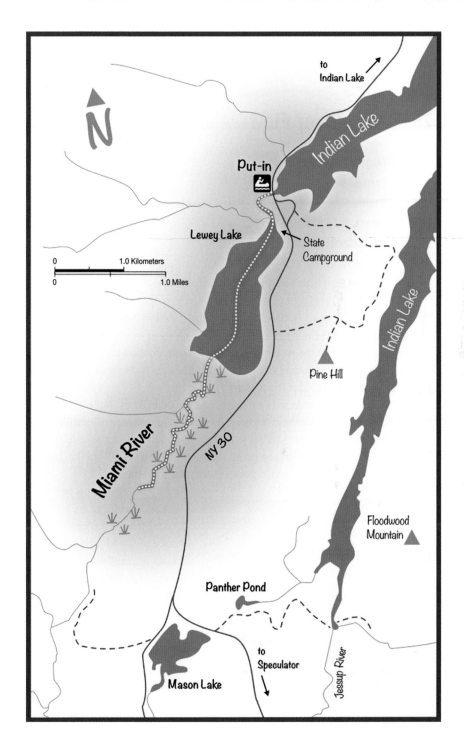

to
Indian Lake

N

Indian Lake

Put-in

Lewey Lake

State
Campground

1.0 Kilometers

1.0 Miles

Indian Lake

Pine Hill

NY 30

Miami River

Floodwood
Mountain

Panther Pond

to
Speculator

Jessup River

Mason Lake

29. Cedar River Flow

Length: 9 miles round-trip
Carries: None
Shuttle: None
Motors: Permitted
Recreational status: Scenic
Put-in: 43°43.572' N, 74°28.377' W
National Geographic map: Northville/Raquette Lake

The wilderness west of Indian Lake contains the tallest Adirondack mountains outside the High Peaks region: a series of summits just under four thousand feet that the writer Barbara McMartin dubbed the Little Great Range. Admiring these giants from a canoe or kayak is just one of the delights of paddling the Cedar River Flow.

The flow is a three-mile impoundment of the Cedar River in the Moose River Plains. Besides mountain scenery, it offers an abundance of birdlife, a mazelike marsh to explore, and, if you're an angler, the chance to catch trout. From the flow, you also can paddle about a mile and a half up the Cedar River to a remote lean-to, a good destination for a picnic.

Pied-billed grebe Photo by Larry Master

The trip begins at Wakely Dam near the Cedar River Road entrance to the Moose River Plains Recreation Area. In summer, the field at the dam may be populated by RV nomads and car-campers. That doesn't mean the flow will be crowded; most of the visitors come to take advantage of the free camping in the Plains. After signing the

The long view on Cedar River Flow. Photo by Mark Bowie

register, paddle across a large bay and then turn east, passing an island, to enter the main part of the flow. The water is shallow and weedy, a deterrent to motorboats. Although anglers occasionally launch small outboards on the flow to fish for brown trout or brookies, your chances of encountering a motor are slim.

Common loons, bald eagles, and ospreys also fish these waters. So do great blue herons, which have established a rookery on the west shore near where the flow starts to narrow. Other waterfowl include black duck, wood duck, mallard, common merganser, American bittern, Wilson's snipe, and pied-billed grebe, according to the guidebook *Adirondack Birding*. In recent years, Canada geese have taken up residence.

As you journey up the flow, look to the east to see the summits of the Little Great Range. Most prominent is 3,786-foot Buell Mountain. To the northwest you can discern another biggie: 3,760-foot Wakely Mountain, topped by a fire tower. Looking across the marsh at the end of the flow, you also enjoy broad views of smaller peaks in the region.

After a few miles, the flow starts to narrow and you soon pass a campsite in the woods on the left. A little beyond here, the Cedar River enters on the

Starting up the flow. Photo by Phil Brown

left, a channel winding through the reeds. If you find yourself among the grassy tussocks at the head of the flow, you've missed the river. That said, you don't want to visit the Cedar River Flow without exploring the labyrinthine tussock swamp—the hideout of herons, ducks, and beavers.

Once on the river, it's an easy upstream paddle to the Carry Lean-to. Keep your eye out for boreal birds such as the gray jay, black-backed woodpecker, boreal chickadee, and yellow-bellied flycatcher. It's possible to paddle beyond the lean-to, but you'll encounter rapids in less than a half-mile. If you want to stretch your legs, take the lean-to trail west a short distance to the Northville-Placid Trail. From there, you could hike for days in either direction.

The return to the flow will go quickly unless you succumb to the temptation to stop at one of the sandy beaches for a swim. Another way to prolong your re-entry into civilization is to poke into Buell Brook. On your return trip, it will be on your right a little past the aforementioned campsite.

DIRECTIONS: From the hamlet of Indian Lake, drive west on NY 28. A few miles outside town, just after crossing the Cedar River, turn left onto Cedar River Road. Drive 12.3 miles (the road eventually turns to dirt) to a large field near Wakely Dam. The put-in is near the dam.

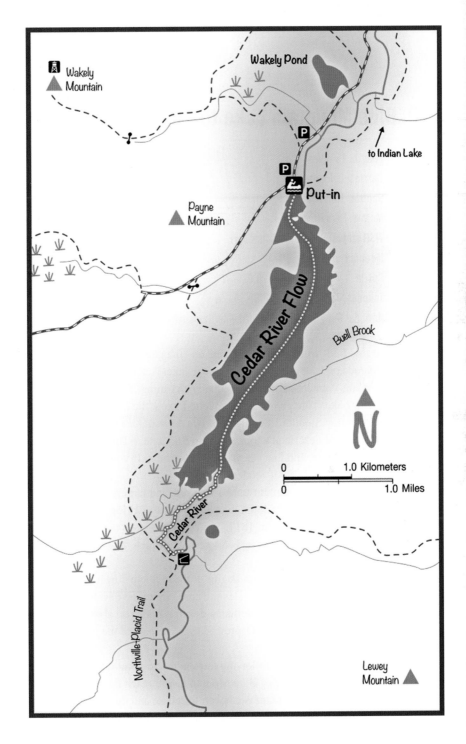

Wakely Pond

🔥 Wakely
▲ Mountain

P

to Indian Lake

P
🛶 Put-in

▲ Payne
Mountain

Cedar River Flow

Buell Brook

N

| 0 | 1.0 Kilometers |
| 0 | 1.0 Miles |

Cedar River

Northville-Placid Trail

Lewey
Mountain ▲

30. Blue Mountain Lake to Raquette Lake

Length: 13 miles
Carries: 0.4 miles
Shuttle: 13.7 miles
Motors: Permitted
WSR status: Scenic (Marion River)
Meander quotient: 31%
Put-in: 43°51.273' N, 74°26.075' W
Takeout: 43°48.798' N, 74°39.399' W
National Geographic map: Northville/Raquette Lake

It's hard to find fault with a trip that begins on "the gem of the smaller lakes" and ends on "the queen of Adirondack lakes," especially when the lakes and streams connecting them are equally charming. The epithets for Blue Mountain Lake ("the gem") and Raquette Lake ("the queen") can be found in Seneca Ray Stoddard's guidebook *The Adirondacks Illustrated* from 1874. Stoddard described a journey from Raquette to Blue, but the trip is often done in reverse, and that's how we'll describe it. If you're worried about fighting west winds, do it Stoddard's way.

At 1,280 acres, Blue Mountain Lake is the first and largest of the three lakes constituting the Eckford Chain, named for Henry Eckford, a naval shipbuilder who surveyed them in 1811. The other two lakes are Eagle and Utowana. The latter is drained by the Marion River, which flows into Raquette Lake.

The trip down the Eckford Chain begins at the municipal beach on the south shore of Blue Mountain Lake. Despite some shoreline development, the lake has not lost its beauty. More than a dozen islands rise above its clear waters. The two largest, Long and Osprey islands, are part of the Forest Preserve.

From the beach, head west, following the south shore, but don't forget to turn around to take in the view of Blue Mountain. You reach the outlet in a mile and a half. The grassy stream is a haven for geese and ducks. Shortly, it passes under a road and enters Eagle Lake. The stone-and-wood bridge was

Blue Mountain Lake from Castle Rock. Photo by Ray Palmer

constructed in 1891 by William West Durant as a memorial to his father, Thomas Durant, the builder of the Union Pacific Rail Road.

Eagle Lake was named by Ned Buntline, a nineteenth-century journalist and dime novelist who built on its north shore a home he called "Eagle's Nest." The Blue Mountain Center, an artists' retreat, now occupies Buntline's spot; otherwise, Eagle's shoreline, though private, is undeveloped.

At the west end of the mile-long lake, you enter a marshy channel filled with water lilies and pickerelweed. In 0.4 miles, it leads to Utowana Lake. Except for a few camps and outbuildings, Utowana also is undeveloped. Nearly all of the shoreline is privately owned, but you'll find some state land at the far end of the lake. The lean-to on the north side is a good place to stop for lunch. It's two miles down the lake and 5.6 miles from your original put-in.

Just beyond the lean-to, the lake narrows and soon ends at a small dam, the start of the Marion River. Take out on the right and follow a 0.4-mile carry trail around rapids. The trail follows the old bed of a tiny railroad that once shuttled passengers between steamboats on the river and the lake. The carry is on private land, so don't leave the trail.

The Marion River meandering toward Raquette Lake. Photo by Carl Heilman II

Many paddlers will think the Marion the best part of the journey. The river winds through one of the largest wetlands in the Adirondacks, a refuge for waterfowl, songbirds, and deer. In season, you can find a variety of wildflowers along the banks, such as turtlehead, cardinal flower, Joe-Pye weed, and purple asters.

The narrow stream has so many turns that, as Stoddard reports, "it would worry eels to follow." Eventually, the river widens and becomes less twisty. After nearly four miles, the Marion reaches a bay on the east side of Raquette Lake. If you need a break, stop at the rock ledges on the right near the river's mouth. They are part of the Forest Preserve. You've now come a total of 10.5 miles.

Keep to the south shore as you head down the bay toward Long Point. In 1.3 miles, after passing St. Williams Church (built in 1890 by W.W. Durant), you reach the main body of the lake. Angle southwest past Big Island (keeping the island on your left) and aim for the hamlet of Raquette Lake on the lake's west shore. Take out at the public beach.

Beware that Raquette Lake and Blue Mountain Lake can be choppy when it's windy. Both lakes see a lot of motorboat traffic in July and August, so this is a trip best done in the off-peak months.

DIRECTIONS: From the T intersection of NY 28 and NY 30 in the hamlet of Blue Mountain Lake, drive south on NY 28 to a public beach on the right. This is the put-in for those doing an east-to-west trip. To reach the takeout, continue 13.1 miles beyond the beach to the turn for Raquette Lake hamlet. Turn right and follow the road for 0.4 miles to a parking lot near the water.

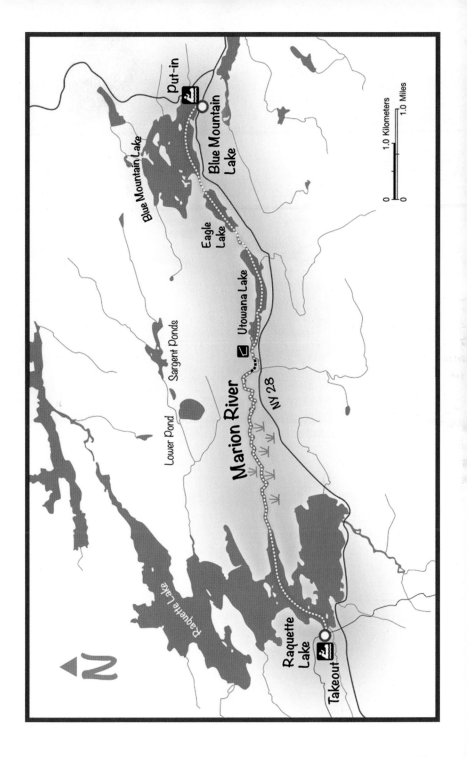

Leaving the put-in behind on Forked Lake. Photo by Phil Brown

31. Forked Lake & Brandreth Lake Outlet

Length: 9 miles round-trip
Carries: 20 yards
Shuttle: No
Motors: Small motorboats on Forked Lake
Meander quotient: 37%
Put-in: 43°53.521' N, 74°35.590' W
National Geographic map: Old Forge/Oswegatchie

For those who can't decide whether they prefer the long views on a big lake or the more intimate beauty of a small stream, this trip offers both.

At 1,248 acres, Forked Lake is one of the larger lakes in the Adirondack Park. Viewed on a map, it looks a little like an upside-down T. The crossbar of the T, where this trip begins, is five and a half miles long and less than a quarter-mile wide.

You can put in either at the Forked Lake State Campground at the east end of the lake (open from late May to early September) or at a concrete dock on the south shore nearly three-quarters of the way up the lake. If you start at the campground, add six miles to the round trip.

From the dock, head due west toward Brandreth Lake Outlet at the far end of the lake. Bear in mind that the north shore, though undeveloped, is privately owned until you get within a half-mile or so of the lake's end. The south shore is Forest Preserve. The lake affords views of Pilgrim Mountain to the northwest and West Mountain to the southwest. If you look back, you can see Blue Mountain and other big peaks in the east.

Forked Lake's north shore is especially attractive, with many tall pines and bedrock outcrops. At 0.4 miles from the put-in, you come to a pine-studded island that's posted against trespass. At 0.75 miles, you pass a few other islands near the south shore. These are in the Forest Preserve.

The marsh at the mouth of Brandreth Lake Outlet is reached after 1.5 miles. Here the stream is broad and sluggish. Don't be surprised to see a great blue heron lurking in the grassy shallows. As you head upstream, you soon encounter beaver dams. If the water is high, you should be able to

Late afternoon in the marsh on Forked Lake. Photo by Phil Brown

paddle over all or most of them.

Once you get beyond the marsh, the stream narrows and becomes more twisty. The evergreen forest and the alders start to close in. About 1.5 miles from the lake, you come to a short stretch constricted by overhanging alders. Don't be discouraged: if you push through, the stream widens again.

A few hundred yards beyond the alder tunnel you come to a short rapid at a bend in the river. Pull off to the left: it's an easy, twenty-yard carry around the rapid. In another quarter-mile, you reach a large beaver dam that you probably will need to drag your boat around.

If the water is high enough, you can continue meandering for another mile through marshland and alder swamp to the foot of a longer rapid, a good place to turn around. You may have to contend with more dams and blowdown to get that far. If you do make it, you will have traveled three miles from Forked Lake. The turnaround is well before the boundary of the private Brandreth Park.

DIRECTIONS: From the junction of NY 28N and NY 30 in Long Lake, drive south on NY 28N/30 for 3.1 miles to North Point Road. Turn right and go 8.7 miles to a dirt road on the right (shortly after crossing the Raquette River). Turn right and follow the road 0.4 miles to its end. If coming from the south, the turn for North Point Road will be on the left 7.7 miles from the intersection of NY 28 and NY 30 in Blue Mountain Lake.

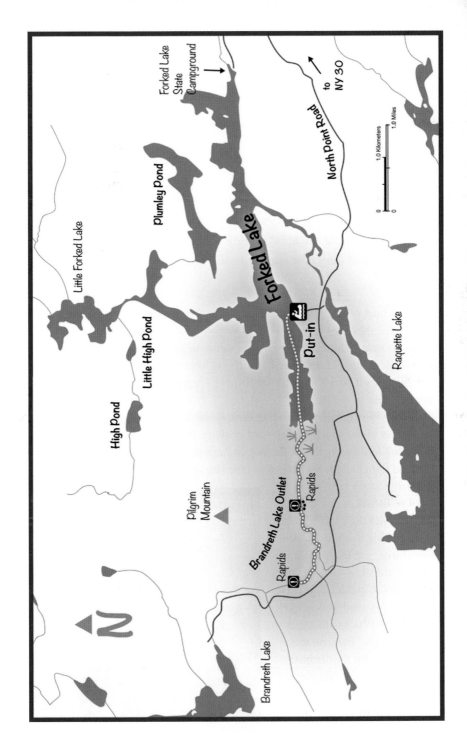

32. South Inlet

....

Length: 4 miles round-trip

Carries: None

Shuttle: No

Motors: Permitted; no-wake zone

Put-in: 43°48.422' N, 74°36.585' W

National Geographic map: Northville/Raquette Lake

South Inlet offers a short, pleasant paddle through boreal bog habitat to a small cascade where you can leave your boat and hike along woodsy trails to Great Camp Sagamore. As its name suggests, South Inlet flows into the south end of Raquette Lake. If you have time, you might want to combine this trip with a paddle up Browns Tract Inlet, a smaller stream on the west side of the lake.

South Inlet is easily accessible from Route 28. At the start, bogs line both sides of the wide channel. Farther along, the evergreen forest creeps down to the shore in places, but bog and marsh always predominate. The wetland flora include rose pogonia, blue flag, cotton grass, sundews, and pitcher plants.

The habitat is rich in bird-life. Besides the usual wetland denizens, such as red-winged blackbirds, you may spot some of the Park's less-common boreal species, including gray jay and black-backed woodpecker. A variety of ducks and other waterfowl also frequent the inlet. Listen for the distinctive *oong-ka-choonk* of the American bittern.

The channel and wetlands

Sundews Photo by Mike Lynch

A paddler's view of the inlet. Photo by Ray Palmer

are broad enough to afford views of nearby peaks on both the upstream paddle and the return trip. A few hundred yards from the put-in, look for a beaver lodge on the right, the first of several you'll pass on the way to the cascade. About a half-mile from the put-in, observe the browse line on the northern white cedars on the left. White-tailed deer love cedar foliage, and in winter they stand on the ice and forage as high up the trees as they can reach. As a result, the cedars are stripped of greenery to a uniform height.

In a mile and a half, the channel makes a big bend to the left and soon comes to a marshy island of sorts. Bear right to stay in the main channel. The stream narrows somewhat as it winds past alder thickets. By this time, you should be able to hear the cascade. After rounding the final bend, you'll see the source of the commotion. Take out at a grassy bank on the left and walk the short distance to the cascade. The flat rocks on the banks are a good place to have a picnic. Don't expect to be overawed: the water drops maybe five feet in two steps.

You can extend your outing by hiking to Great Camp Sagamore. Once a

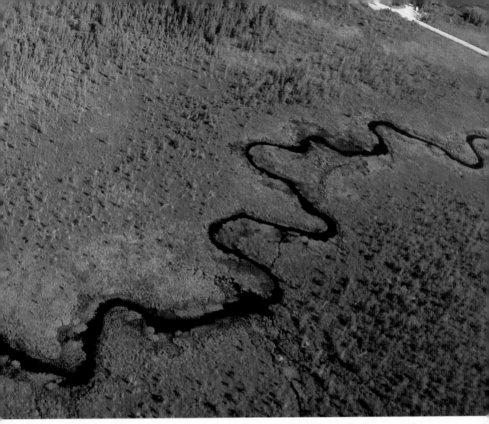

The winding stream. Photo by Phil Brown

retreat of the Vanderbilt family, the rustic compound is now maintained by the nonprofit Sagamore Institute. Follow a trail (marked by blue disks) along the stream for a mile and a half to Sagamore Road. Turn left and walk about a half-mile to the Great Camp. On the return hike, you can follow a trail on the opposite side of the stream, but when you get to the cascade, you'll have to wade through the water to get back to your starting point.

DIRECTIONS: From the junction of NY 28 and NY 28/30 in Blue Mountain Lake, drive west on NY 28 for 10.8 miles to a large pull-off just before the bridge over South Inlet. If coming from the opposite direction, you'll reach the pull-off 2.6 miles past the turn for the hamlet of Raquette Lake. Put in on the south side of the highway.

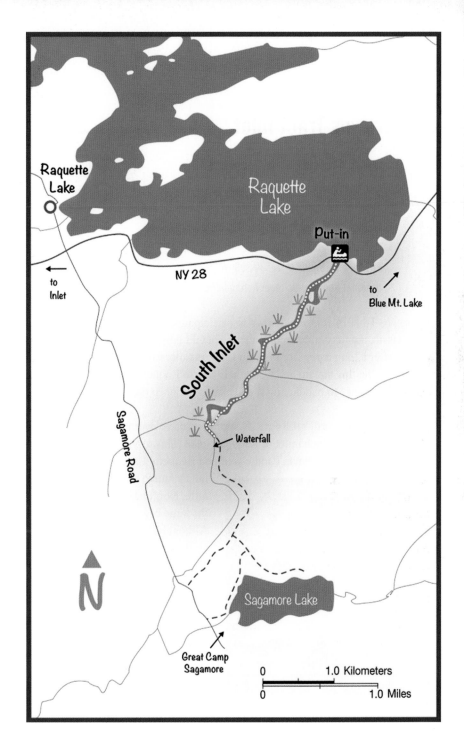

Raquette Lake

Raquette Lake

Put-in

NY 28

to Inlet

to Blue Mt. Lake

South Inlet

Sagamore Road

Waterfall

N

Sagamore Lake

Great Camp Sagamore

| 0 | | 1.0 Kilometers |
| 0 | | 1.0 Miles |

33. Browns Tract Inlet

Length: 6 miles round-trip
Carries: None
Shuttle: No
Motors: Permitted
Meander quotient: 35%
Put-in: 43°48.798' N, 74°39.399' W
National Geographic map: Northville/Raquette Lake

Browns Tract Inlet is well known to participants in the Adirondack Canoe Classic, a ninety-mile race that starts in Old Forge and ends in Saranac Lake. After a long carry from Eighth Lake, paddlers are grateful to slip their boats into the tiny stream and wend their way to Raquette Lake. Fortunately, it's not necessary to paddle ninety miles to experience the charms of this wild waterway.

After turning north off Route 28, motorists drive over Browns Tract Inlet on the way to the hamlet of Raquette Lake. This trip starts at the hamlet's small public beach. Paddle south on Raquette Lake to reach the inlet's mouth in just a quarter-mile. Don't be discouraged by the large beaver dam at the start. Although there are several dams on the inlet, you can get over most of them without exiting the boat. The dams, however, make the stream impractical for travel by motorboat.

Indeed, Browns Tract Inlet is a world away from the jet-skis and powerboats on the big lake. No wakes or whitecaps here. Usually, the surface is as

Fragrant water lily Photo by Phil Brown

Big sky over Browns Tract Inlet. Photo by Phil Brown

smooth as a mirror, adorned with water lilies, pickerelweed, and other aquatic plants. The stream winds through a large peatland that supports a suite of bog vegetation: leatherleaf, pitcher plants, sundews, tamarack trees, and roses.

The habitat attracts a number of boreal birds. Retired forest ranger Gary Lee, co-author of *Adirondack Birding*, reports seeing black-backed woodpeckers, gray jays, Lincoln's sparrows, and olive-sided flycatchers, sometimes winging across the water. American bittern and Wilson's snipe dwell in the marshy areas.

About a mile up the inlet, there is a good view of the cliffs on Fox Mountain to the north. At 1.5 miles, the forest starts to close in, with pines and cedars growing near the shore. Farther on, you pass stands of dead

Following the boardwalk to Browns Tract Inlet. Photo by Nancie Battaglia

evergreens, victims of flooding. At 2.75 miles, you arrive at a boardwalk—the end of the carry from Eighth Lake. It's possible to go a little bit farther, but the stream is shallow and narrow.

Apart from the boardwalk, you won't encounter any development on Browns Tract Inlet. The stream lies entirely within the Forest Preserve. Its only flaw is its proximity to Route 28. Although you don't see the road, you do hear cars occasionally.

Because of its twists and turns, Browns Tract Inlet often frustrates paddlers competing in the Adirondack Canoe Classic. The lesson is obvious: slow down and smell the wild roses.

DIRECTIONS: From NY 28, turn north on County 2 and follow it 0.4 miles to a public parking lot in the hamlet of Raquette Lake. The turn is next to a power station. If you're coming from the north or east, it's 13.4 miles from the junction of NY 28 and NY 30 in Blue Mountain Lake. From the south or east, it's about 12 miles from the hamlet of Inlet. Launch your canoe from the beach near the parking lot.

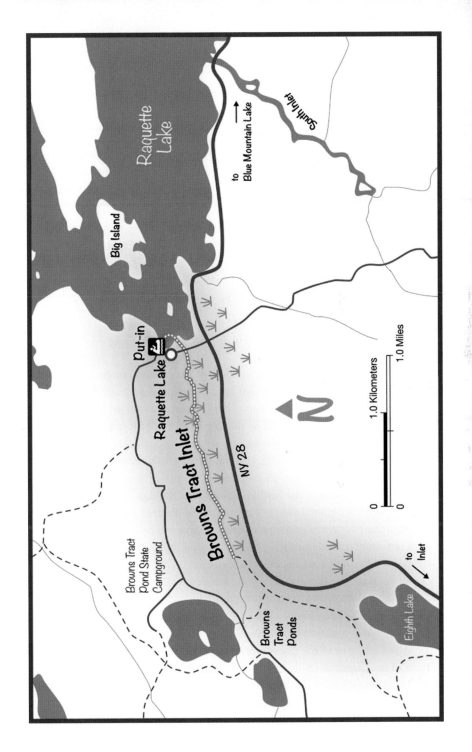

34. North Branch of the Moose

Length: Up to 12.4 miles

Carries: 0.25 miles

Shuttle: 9.1 miles

Motors: Permitted

WSR status: Recreational

Meander quotient: 48%

Put-in: 43°45.810' N, 74°55.225' W

Takeout: 43°41.679' N, 74°59.909' W

National Geographic map: Old Forge/Oswegatchie

The North Branch of the Moose offers paddlers an easy escape from the hubbub of Old Forge—not far but nevertheless a world away from the hamlet's shops, restaurants, and bars. There are several options for a downstream meander, the longest a 12.4-mile trip from Carter Road to a takeout on the Middle Branch of the Moose. If you lack a second car or don't want to bicycle between the endpoints, you can arrange a shuttle with either Mountainman Outdoor Supply Company or Tickner's Canoe.

For most of this trip, the North Branch winds through alder swamps and marshes, with occasional views of nearby peaks. Retired forest ranger Gary Lee says the river corridor harbors an astounding variety of birds, including such uncommon northern species as the gray jay, black-backed woodpecker, olive-sided flycatcher, and boreal chickadee.

At the start, the shoreline is mostly wooded, with some steep sandy banks, but eventually the river enters the alders and becomes more serpentine. You need to keep an eye on the current to make sure you don't make a wrong turn into a watery cul-de-sac.

Although most of the river corridor is privately owned, there are few signs of development until the end of the trip. At 0.85 miles, you come to a steel bridge that's used in winter by snowmobilers. At 1.0 mile, you pass a lean-to on the left bank, but it's on private land and not open to the public.

The North Street bridge is reached at 5.7 miles. If you want to do a

Hung up in the shallows on the North Branch of the Moose. Photo by Phil Brown

shorter trip, you can take out here. Another option is to put in here and take out in Old Forge for a 7.8-mile trip. If you choose the second option, bear in the mind that you face a quarter-mile carry farther downriver. Also, the river becomes more developed as it approaches and then passes through the hamlet.

Below North Street, the land along the left shore all the way to the Middle Branch lies in the public Forest Preserve. If you want to have lunch or take a swim, feel free to stop on this side of the river. There are many sandy beaches on the bends that make ideal picnic spots.

At nine miles or so, you may notice railroad tracks above the right shore. At 9.4 miles, you come to a three-way junction. Bear left here, or you'll end up traveling in a circle back to the same spot—which some people might find an amusing diversion.

Soon after, you should hear rapids.

Boreal chickadee Photo by Larry Master

Crossing the river on the carry. Photo by Phil Brown

A sign on the left bank at 9.6 miles marks the start of the carry. Follow the trail to a wooden bridge, cross the river, turn left, and put in below the rapids. Shortly, the fairways of a golf course appear along the right bank. Then traffic on Route 28 becomes more audible. At 11.3 miles, just before the highway, you reach the Middle Branch.

If you arranged a shuttle with Mountainman or Tickner's your trip is almost over. Mountainman, located on Route 28, has a dock near the rivers' confluence, and Tickner's is just a short distance up the Middle Branch. Other paddlers should continue downriver, passing under Route 28, to the public takeout on Green Bridge Road. It's about a mile from the confluence. In this final stretch, you pass under power lines and see a number of houses, but the ducks seem unfazed by the development.

DIRECTIONS: From NY 28 in Thendara, just east of the railroad trestle, drive south on Beech Street for 0.4 miles to the bridge over the Middle Branch of the Moose (en route Beech Street turns into Green Bridge Road). Leave a car on the far side of the bridge in the lot on the right. This is the takeout. To reach the put-in, return to NY 28. Turn right and go 7.1 miles to Rondaxe Road. Turn left and go 1.5 miles to Carter Road. Bear right and go 0.5 miles to the bridge over the North Branch of the Moose. To reach the alternative takeout/put-in on North Street, turn onto North Street from NY 28 and drive 1.4 miles to the bridge. North Street begins just west of the Enchanted Forest amusement park.

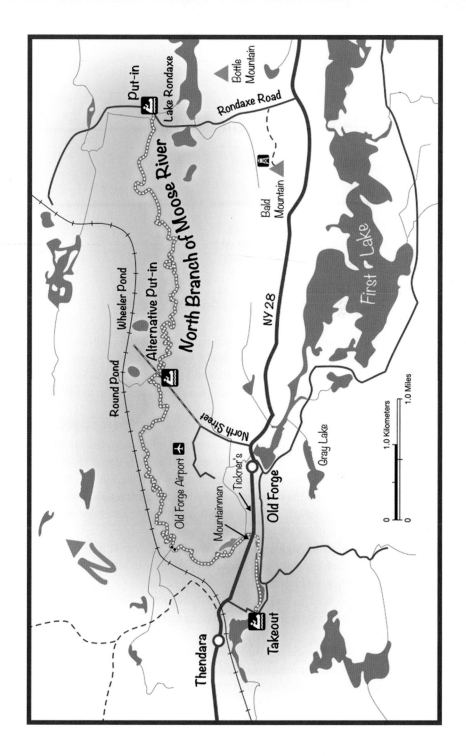

Put-in

Lake Rondaxe

Bottle Mountain

Rondaxe Road

Bald Mountain

North Branch of Moose River

Alternative Put-in

Wheeler Pond

Round Pond

First Lake

NY 28

Old Forge Airport

North Street

Mountainman

Tickner's

Old Forge

Gray Lake

Thendara

Takeout

1.0 Kilometers

1.0 Miles

35. Middle Branch of the Moose

Length: 12 miles round-trip
Carries: 20 yards
Shuttle: No
Motors: Permitted
Put-in: 43°41.679' N, 74°59.909' W
WSR status: Recreational
Meander quotient: 37%
National Geographic map: Old Forge/Oswegatchie

Canoeists love cruising downriver. Paddling back against the current? Not so much. That's one reason the shuttle was invented. Of course, a shuttle usually means taking two cars and a lot of driving back and forth. If canoeing the Middle Branch of the Moose, though, you can avoid the shuttle as well as the upstream slog.

Thanks to a partnership between Tickner's Canoe in Old Forge and Adirondack Scenic Railroad, paddlers can travel seven miles down the Middle Branch and ride the train back. The "River and Rail" trips begin at Tickner's dock, a short distance upstream from the confluence with the Moose's North Branch. Later in the day, the train picks up the paddlers and returns them to Old Forge (Thendara depot). Tickner's then drives them the short distance back to the store.

If you want to do the Middle Branch without buying a train ticket, you have the usual options: paddle back upriver or arrange a shuttle. The latter will require paddling through rapids to get to a legal takeout.

Of course, you need go down the river only as far you like. Many families and casual paddlers opt for an easy flatwater trip to Lock and Dam— only a mile each way.

The public put-in for the Middle Branch is on Green Bridge Road in Old Forge. This is about a mile from Tickner's, as the river flows. From here, it's about six miles to the first rapids. At the start, the broad river twists and turns through a marsh. Although homes and busy Route 28 are close by,

The wooden dam on the Middle Branch of the Moose. Photo by Nancy L. Ford

the waterfowl don't seem to mind: you should see ducks, herons, and other birds. Shortly, you leave the hamlet behind, but you can still hear highway traffic. After 1.1 miles, you arrive at Lock and Dam, a wooden spillway.

The wilder stretches of the Middle Branch lie ahead, so even if you don't intend to paddle all the way to the rapids, you should continue at least a short distance beyond the dam. To carry around the dam, take out at an obvious landing on the left bank. The carry is only twenty yards or so.

Below the dam the river is much narrower as it winds through the forest. Farther downstream, the forest gives way in places to alder swamp and marshland. You may see a great blue heron stalking the shallows or an American bittern hiding in the grass. The marshy flatlands also offer occasional views of neighboring hills. If you're not doing a through trip, you might want to turn around within a few miles of the dam, after you've had your fill of the scenery. Although the current is mostly gentle, your arms will feel it on the way back.

If you continue downstream, you'll come to a short rapid nearly six miles from your initial put-in. A sign on the left marks the start of the carry trail. The portage is a tenth of a mile. Afterward, you need only cross the river to reach the pickup spot for the train.

Heading downriver by boat and train. Photo by Nancy L. Ford

The rail stop is just a few hundred yards up the tracks from the end of Minnehaha Road. Unfortunately, carrying your canoe down the tracks is illegal. Also, you'd need to cross a small piece of private land to get from the tracks to the road. Otherwise, flatwater paddlers could do the Middle Moose as a through trip. As things stand, through travelers must continue downriver through class II rapids, passing under a railroad trestle.

And where to take out? Although paddlers often access the river along Scusa Road, the bank is private property. If you have permission, exit here. Otherwise, take out on Forest Preserve land along Route 28 a little south of Scusa Road. Beware that Nelson Falls, a class IV drop, lurks downriver not far from this takeout. If you come to another railroad trestle, you've gone too far; the falls lie just ahead.

DIRECTIONS: From NY 28 in Thendara, turn south on Beech Street (just east of the railroad trestle) and drive 0.5 miles to a parking area on the right. This is just past the bridge over the river. Note that Beech Street turns into Green Bridge Road before you reach the river. For the best put-in, carry your boat back across the bridge and down the small embankment on the right.

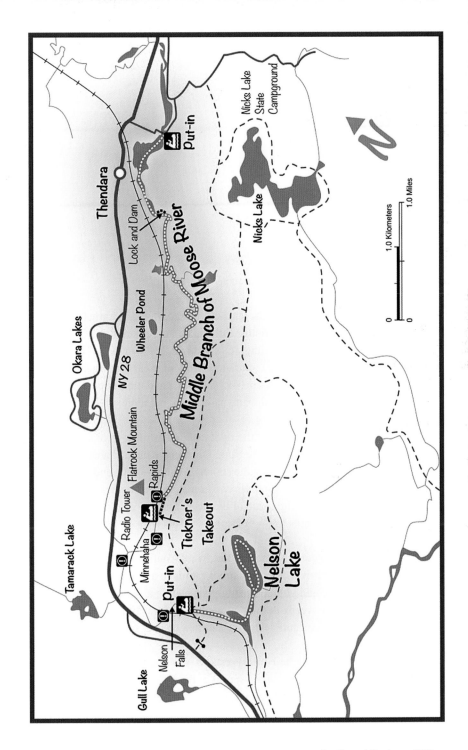

Nicks Lake State Campground

Nicks Lake

Put-in

Thendara

Lock and Dam

Okara Lakes

Wheeler Pond

NY 28

Middle Branch of Moose River

Flatrock Mountain

Radio Tower

Rapids

Tickner's Takeout

Minnehaha

Tamarack Lake

Nelson Lake

Put-in

Nelson Falls

Gull Lake

N

1.0 Kilometers
1.0 Miles

0   0

36. Nelson Lake

....

Length: 3.5 miles
Carries: 0.35 miles
Shuttle: No
Motors: Permitted
WSR status: Recreational
Put-in: 43°38.811' N, 75°04.728' W
National Geographic map: Old Forge/Oswegatchie

Thank heaven for the carry at the start of this trip. It must be what keeps the crowds away from this pristine little lake in the Black River Wild Forest. The portage notwithstanding, the short paddle down the Middle Branch of the Moose to Nelson Lake is an excellent excursion for families or anyone looking for a quick nature fix. It's wilder and more secluded than the popular trip to Lock and Dam, another short paddle on the Middle Branch.

You begin at a side channel of the river just downstream from some rapids. Indian poke grows along the bank. Once in the main channel, you'll see mostly marsh vegetation along the shores: wetland shrubs and grassy tussocks. Within a half-mile, you pass two homes: one a beaver lodge, the other a small camp on the right side of the river. You may also notice a side channel on the left that cuts through the marsh. This is an optional route for the return trip.

At 0.6 miles, you come to the shallow, weedy outlet of Nelson Lake. (If you continue downriver, you encounter rapids in a few hundred yards.) In summer, you may find yourself using your paddle as a pole to push your way through the weeds in the outlet. But your travail is brief, for the channel soon widens and deepens. Within a quarter-mile of the river, you're on the lake.

Nelson lies entirely in the Forest Preserve. You can easily make a circuit of the lake. Perhaps the most scenic spot is at the far end, where a slab of gray-pink rock slips into the water. From here you can look across the lake

A bedrock shelf on Nelson Lake. Photo by Phil Brown

at the wooded hills in the distance. It's a good place for a picnic or a swim.

If you follow the east shore on the return, you may notice an old picnic table with a bench missing. (Also look for a large boulder on shoreline.) If you want to stretch your legs, land here and follow an unmarked path a short way to an old woods road that serves as a snowmobile trail.

After leaving Nelson Lake, look for a channel on the right before the outlet reaches the river. You can follow the channel along the marsh and then cut left back to the river. It's a minor variation on a pretty melody.

DIRECTIONS: From the bridge over the Moose River at McKeever, drive northeast on NY 28 for 2.8 miles to a dirt road on the right marked by a DEC sign. If you're coming from the opposite direction, the turn off NY 28 is 5.7 miles past the railroad depot in Thendara. The dirt road quickly ends at a parking area. From there, portage along a woods road (gated), bearing left at a fork reached at 0.1 miles. At 0.3 miles you cross railroad tracks. A short path to the right leads to a put-in on a grassy bank below rapids.

37. The Inlet on Big Moose Lake

Length: 5 miles round-trip
Carries: None
Shuttle: No
Motors: Permitted
Put-in: 43°49.635' N, 74°50.298' W
National Geographic Map: Old Forge/Oswegatchie

Big Moose Lake served as the poster child for acid rain after pollution from distant power plants killed most of the lake's fish. In recent years, thanks to stronger environmental regulations, the acidity has abated and the fish are making a recovery—so much so that loons now nest on the lake. Paddlers who visit the marsh in Big Moose's northeast bay, known as the Inlet, can see other waterbirds as well, such as great blue herons, mergansers, and mallards. And those who combine the paddle with a hike into the Pigeon Lake Wilderness will have a chance to see a variety of woodland birds.

West winds can whip up a chop on the 1,265-acre lake, so wait for a calm day. For the shortest crossing to the Inlet, start at the Big Moose Property Owners Association dock on the south side of the lake. Paddle northeast for a mile to the entrance of the northeast bay. A sign warns motorboats not to exceed five miles an hour. Heading up the bay, you pass a landing on the left after about 0.4 miles. This is the start of the trail to Gull Lakes. It leads in 1.2 miles to a lean-to on Upper Gull Lake, a good spot for a swim. The trail

Common merganser Photo by Larry Master

The entrance to the Inlet on Big Moose Lake. Photo by Phil Brown

skirts the south shore of Lower Gull on the way.

Beyond the Gull Lakes landing, paddle up the channel through a large marsh. In addition to waterfowl, you may see belted kingfishers and cedar waxwings. As you near the end of the bay, look for a narrow channel that winds through the grasses. It leads in 0.3 miles to a trailhead at the mouth of Andy's Creek—about 2.5 miles from the put-in.

From the landing you can hike to a lean-to upstream on the creek or another lean-to on Lower Sister Lake. The trail for both starts out the same. After 0.2 miles, you come to a junction. Turn left for the Andy's Creek lean-to, reached in another 0.3 miles. Continue straight for Lower Sister Lake. At 3.3 miles from Big Moose Lake, you arrive at a lean-to on a rock ledge near the shore. The trails to Gull Lakes, Andy's Creek, and Lower Sister pass through habitat that harbors boreal birds such as gray

A common loon with chicks. Photo by Larry Master

jay, boreal chickadee, and black-backed woodpecker. You also can hear a variety of wood warblers.

On the return paddle, you may want to take a detour into East Bay to visit Russian Lake. From the East Bay landing, a trail leads 0.7 miles to a lean-to overlooking the pretty lake. History buffs might want to see South Bay as well. This is where Chester Gillette drowned his pregnant girlfriend in 1906, a murder that inspired Theodore Dreiser's novel *An American Tragedy*. The movie *A Place in the Sun*, starring Elizabeth Taylor and and Montgomery Cliff, was based on the novel.

DIRECTIONS: From NY 28 in the hamlet of Eagle Bay, drive north on Big Moose Road for 3.9 miles to Higby Road. Turn right and go 1.6 miles to a parking lot at a dock owned by the Big Moose Property Owners Association.

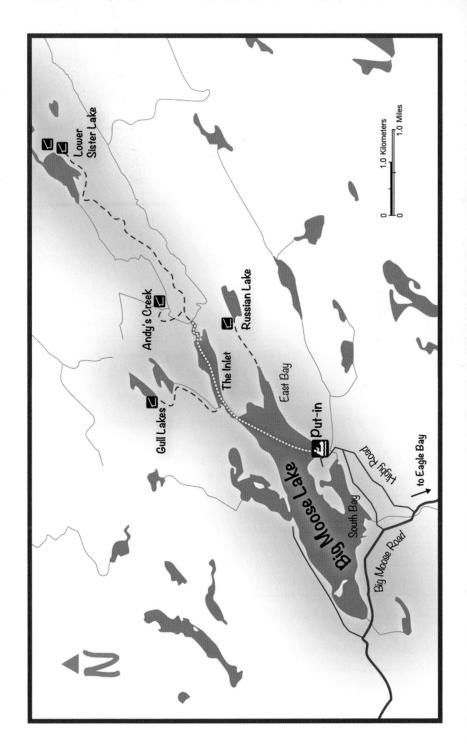

N

Lower Sister Lake

Andy's Creek

Russian Lake

Gull Lakes

The Inlet

East Bay

Big Moose Lake

Put-in

to Eagle Bay

Higby Road

South Bay

Big Moose Road

1.0 Kilometers
1.0 Miles
0
0

38. Beaver River Canoe Route

Length: Up to 15.2 miles
Carries: 7 totaling 2.8 miles
Shuttle: 18.1 miles
Motors: Permitted
Put-in: 43°52.233' N, 75°08.240' W
Takeout: 43°55.965' N, 75°22.117' W
National Geographic map: Old Forge/Oswegatchie

Paddling the Beaver River Canoe Route is closer to pond hopping than river tripping. If you do the whole thing, you'll visit nine impoundments connected by six carries. It's best done as a one-way downriver excursion, leaving a second car or a bicycle at the takeout. If you opt for a bike shuttle, note that much of your pedaling will be on dirt roads.

Brookfield Power maintains the canoe route, including carry trails, picnic sites, and campsites. It starts at Beaver Lake, a few miles below Stillwater Reservoir, and ends at High Falls Reservoir just west of the Adirondack Park. You can shorten the trip from fifteen to eleven miles by ending at Taylorville Reservoir. For an even shorter outing, with no carries, you could do a round-trip from Eagle Reservoir to Beaver Lake.

Don't expect to find nature in its pristine glory. Seasonal homes have been built on most of the reservoirs, and especially in summer you may encounter a few motorboats or jet skis. In addition, you'll see all the infrastructure necessary for generating hydropower: dams, turbine houses, water pipes, utility lines, access roads. That said, the canoe route offers plenty of wild scenery and the opportunity to view loons, herons, ducks, mergansers, and a variety of other birds, including bald eagles.

From the Moshier Road parking lot, there is a 0.3-mile carry, crossing Sunday Creek, to the first put-in on Beaver Lake. Heading downstream, you soon come to a marsh. The channel widens as you approach the lake proper, with more marshland along the shores. The guidebook *Adirondack Birding* reports that Wilson's snipe, American bittern, Virginia rail, and other waterfowl inhabit the Beaver Lake marshes.

The whitewater gorge below Eagle Reservoir. Photo by Donald Cochran

Stay close to the right (and wilder) shore as you cross the lake to the outlet channel, about two miles from the put-in. Except for some power lines reached at 2.4 miles, the broad channel is undeveloped, with several piney islands. At 3.5 miles, you arrive at one of the larger islands, featuring a long rock wall that rises straight out of the water. Soon after, you can see the dam ahead. This part of the canoe route is known as Eagle Reservoir, though it's hard to tell where the channel ends and the reservoir begins. Take out on the left just before the dam, at 4.1 miles.

You now have a 0.8-mile carry to Upper Soft Maple Reservoir, nearly all of it along a dirt road that parallels a gorge used by whitewater kayakers. At the halfway point is a resting bench with a stand to hold your canoe. The put-in is just below the Eagle Falls powerhouse.

Upper Soft Maple is one of the larger and busier reservoirs. Brookfield Power maintains campsites on a large peninsula on the north shore and on two islands. Several camps exist along the south shore. When you get on the open water, head toward the large embankment on the western shore. Just before reaching the shore, turn left to pass a dam, about 1.3 miles from the put-in. You are now in a short channel that leads to Lower Soft Maple Reservoir. The power company operates a small campground on the point on the left. Continuing down the channel, you exit the Adirondack Park and enter Lower Soft Maple, a serene reservoir, less than a mile long, that remains largely undeveloped.

After taking out at the far end of Lower Soft Maple, you have a 0.25-mile carry to Effley Falls Reservoir (turn right when you reach the dirt road). The put-in is near another powerhouse. The reservoir widens as you head downriver, narrows as you turn right to round a peninsula, then widens again as you head toward the dam at the west end, reached at 1.4 miles from the put-in. Take out to the right of the sloping bedrock at the water's edge.

A 0.2-mile trail leads to Elmer Falls Reservoir, a narrow water body with cedars lining its north shore and—a welcome change—no houses in sight. Alas, it's only 0.6 miles to the takeout. Look for it on the right shore. The bank is steep, so disembarking can be tricky. A 0.1-mile trail climbs over a ridge to the eastern arm of Taylorville Reservoir.

The next half-mile is one of the wilder and more attractive sections of the canoe route. Put in at the large pool below Elmer Falls, where water spills in steps over bedrock slabs. You then enter the reservoir's riverine arm, lined with grasses and evergreens. The current picks up as the water squeezes between two bedrock shelves; ride it into the open water and then aim for the pine-studded island in the middle of the pond. The takeout is 0.4 miles beyond the island, to the right of the dam and bedrock outcrops. This is 1.5 miles from the put-in.

Brookfield Power maintains a picnic site near the takeout. Since it's accessible by car, you may want to end your trip here. Those who continue face a carry of almost a mile along roads to Belfort Reservoir (with two benches and canoe stands en route).

Once on Belfort Reservoir, you're back in civilization. A half-mile paddle ends at a paved highway in the hamlet of Belfort. While paddling the reservoir, beware of submerged rocks. After taking out, cross the road, turn right, and pick up a carry trail that leads 0.2 miles to the grassy banks of the Beaver River.

Over the next 1.5 miles, the Beaver actually resembles a river as it passes through woods and farmland on its way to High Falls Reservoir. The fields and the water attract huge flocks of geese. When you reach the reservoir, you'll notice a few islands to the right (there are campsites on the islands). Pass between the islands to reach the takeout on the northwest shore.

DIRECTIONS: From the junction of NY 126 and NY 812 in Croghan, drive north on 812 for 3.4 miles to Old State Road. Turn right and go 0.9 miles to the High Falls Reservoir parking lot on the right. This is the takeout. To reach the put-in, continue on Old State Road for 1.5 miles to County 10 in Belfort. Turn right, cross the river, and take the first left onto Effley Falls Road. Go 4.4 miles to a T intersection at Soft Maple Road. Turn left and go 1.7 miles to Adsit Trail. Turn left and go 6.5 miles to Buck Point Road. Turn right and go 0.5 miles to a three-way intersection. Turn left and go 2.1 miles to Moshier Road. Turn left and go 0.6 miles to a parking lot on the right. The carry trail begins across the road from the lot.

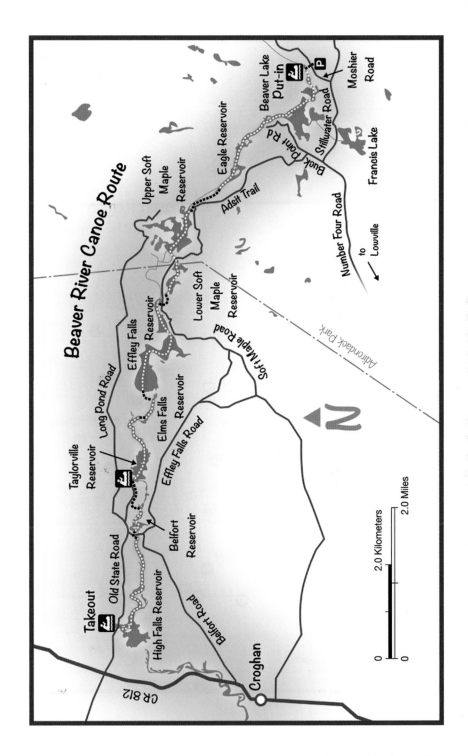

Beaver River Canoe Route

Beaver Lake Put-in

Moshier Road

Stillwater Road

Francis Lake

Buck Point Rd

Eagle Reservoir

Adsit Trail

Number Four Road

to Lowville

Upper Soft Maple Reservoir

Lower Soft Maple Reservoir

Soft Maple Road

Adirondack Park

Effley Falls Reservoir

Long Pond Road

Elms Falls Reservoir

Effley Falls Road

Taylorville Reservoir

Belfort Reservoir

Old State Road

Takeout

High Falls Reservoir

Belfort Road

Croghan

CR 812

N

2.0 Kilometers

2.0 Miles

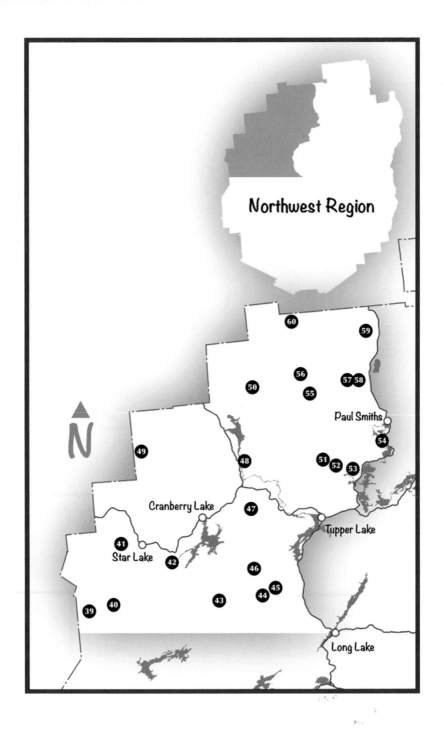

Northwest Region

Bog Islands at Madawaska Flow. Photo by Phil Brown

NORTHWEST REGION

The put-in along the Jakes Pond Trail. Photo by Phil Brown

39. West Branch of the Oswegatchie

Length: 4 miles for first trip; up to 7 miles for second
Carries: 1 to 4, depending on itinerary
Shuttle: No
Motors: Permitted
WSR status: Scenic
Meander quotient: 41%
Put-in: 43°59.669' N, 75°10.747' W
National Geographic map: Old Forge/Oswegatchie

The West Branch of the Oswegatchie is not a river that reveals its wild side to just anyone, but if you're willing to drive to the middle of nowhere and carry your canoe a quarter-mile, you'll get a reward—nearly two miles of mostly level water in a marshy floodplain.

Only two miles? It's not a lot, but you can easily fit into the same day another flatwater excursion that includes a visit to Iowa Falls, one of the region's more spectacular waterfalls. Altogether, you can paddle up to 11.4 miles on the two trips.

En route to Bergrens Clearing, your first starting point, you drive over the West Branch three times, and any of these bridges can serve as a put-in for your second trip. The clearing is 0.7 miles past the third bridge on the road. The carry is along the Jakes Pond Trail. The path dips to cross a small stream and comes to a T-intersection in less than a tenth of a mile. Turn left and follow the trail over bedrock slabs to a footbridge at 0.25 miles.

Below the bridge, the river plunges through a series of pretty cascades. You want to put in at the pool above the bridge and head upstream. Although this part of the river flows through private land, you have the right to paddle here. As you wind upriver, you will see numerous DEC signs indicating that this is a public fishing stream.

Wetland shrubs, sedges, and tamaracks grow in the floodplain, but hardwoods dominate the higher ground and the hills in the distance. Don't be too surprised if you see wild azaleas in late May or early June. Paul Jamieson

Iowa Falls on the West Branch of the Oswegatchie. Photo by Phil Brown

says in *Adirondack Canoe Waters: North Flow* that the flowers bloom in several spots along the river.

A half-mile from the put-in, you come to a large beaver dam, but you may be able to paddle around it. A beaver lodge is on the other side. At almost a mile, you pass large angular boulders in the water and soon reach shallow riffles below a footbridge. Walk your boat up the shallows and carry left around the bridge. This is the second bridge on the Jakes Pond Trail. If you were to follow the trail, you'd reach a third bridge over the West Branch in 1.2 miles. Unfortunately, you won't be able to get that far in your canoe.

Get back in your boat in the large pool above the bridge. The river soon narrows as you meander upstream through alders and sedge meadows. If you make a wrong turn, you might flush a bittern or mallard from a watery cul-de-sac. Jamieson says the showiest display of azaleas is found a third of a mile above the bridge, on the left.

At 1.75 miles from your original put-in, boulders block further progress. Don't bother to carry around them into the pool on the other side: longer rapids lie just around the bend.

Once back at the car, you have several options for the second trip, ranging from 1.3 to 7.4 miles, including carries. You can put in at or near any of the three bridges crossed on the way to Bergrens Clearing. We'll describe the longest trip and suggest shorter variations. Whatever you do, be

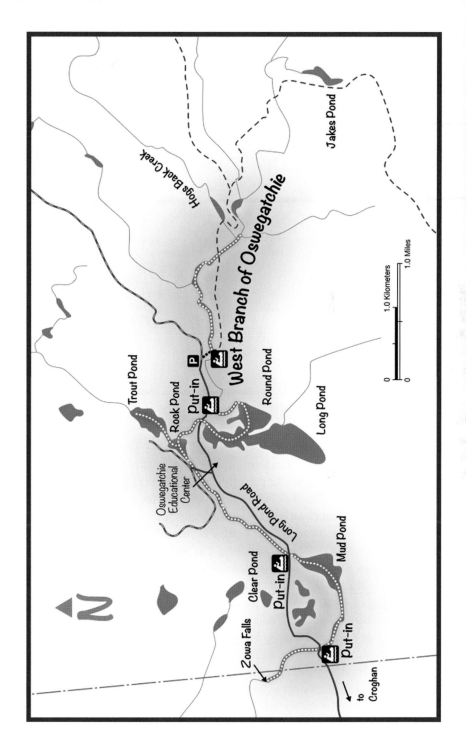

N

Jakes Pond

Hogs Back Creek

West Branch of Oswegatchie

Trout Pond

Rock Pond

Put-in

P

Round Pond

Long Pond

Oswegatchie
Educational
Center

Long Pond Road

Mud Pond

Clear Pond

Put-in

Put-in

Zowa Falls

to
Croghan

1.0 Kilometers

1.0 Miles

0   0

View from above Iowa Falls. Photo by Phil Brown

sure to include Iowa Falls in your itinerary.

The last bridge before the clearing crosses the outlet of Long Pond. You could put in right here (the property is owned by the Oswegatchie Educational Center, which allows public access), but for a more interesting start, carry your boat down a dirt road that begins just east of the bridge. In a tenth of a mile, it comes close to the West Branch. Put in and paddle downstream for 0.4 miles to Round Pond. The river is shallow, so you may scrape bottom in low water. Cross Round Pond into Long Pond and follow the outlet to Rock Pond. The outlet also contains shallow riffles.

From Rock Pond, you can take a detour to Trout Pond, which is free of all development. To get there, paddle to the north end of Rock and carry over a beaver dam and a floating bridge.

Upon returning to Rock Pond, head to the southwest corner to pick up the West Branch again. The river passes through hemlock stands and marshes. You may encounter more shallow riffles as well as deadfalls. After paddling under the second bridge on Long Pond Road, you enter Mud Pond. Once you get away from the road, the pond is wild and scenic.

Traveling in an arc, you eventually come to an island next to an old dam that you must carry around. Just beyond the island you pass under the first bridge on Long Pond Road. Take out on the right before a waterfall and carry downhill to a put-in.

It's a pleasant half-mile paddle through marsh grasses and alders to a footbridge at the top of Iowa Falls. Take out on the right before the bridge to enjoy the scenery. From the bridge, you can watch as the West Branch rushes beneath your feet and plunges over pink-gray slabs of bedrock. Far below, the waters gather in a dark pool before winding away through lush green meadows. To view the waterfall from its base, hike down a steep path on the right side of the river. When you've had your fill, paddle back to Long Pond Road.

The long version of this trip entails 7.1 miles of paddling, plus three short carries. It takes in five ponds and two waterfalls. You can shorten the trip to 4.7 miles of paddling and two carries by skipping Round Pond and Trout Pond. There is a 2.9-mile shuttle at the end.

There are two options for shorter trips:

Start at Mud Pond. This variation involves 2.5 miles of paddling. At the end, you'll need to walk, bicycle, or drive a mile back to your starting point. Park on the south side of the road near the second bridge. A path on the other side of the road leads to a public dock.

If seeing the falls is your only objective, start at the first bridge. The parking

American bittern Photo by Larry Master

area for this trip is on the north side of the road at the head of the first waterfall. This round-trip entails only a mile of paddling, with a short carry at the beginning and end.

DIRECTIONS: From NY 812 in Croghan, turn east on Belfort Road and drive 3.7 miles to Long Pond Road in Belfort. Turn right at this T-intersection and go 2.1 miles to an informational kiosk, where Long Pond Road makes a 90-degree turn to the left. Make the turn and continue on Long Pond Road for 8.2 miles to a large clearing. On the way, you cross the West Branch three times: at 4.6 miles, 6.8 miles, and 7.5 miles past the 90-degree turn.

40. Alder Bed Flow

Length: 8.6 miles round-trip
Carries: 500 yards
Shuttle: No
Motors: Prohibited
WSR status: Wild
Meander quotient: 45%
Put-in: 43°59.924' N, 75°03.696' W
National Geographic map: Old Forge/Oswegatchie

Beautiful things are difficult—an ancient maxim that can be applied to Alder Bed Flow. This lovely still-water on the Middle Branch of the Oswegatchie is as remote and wild as any destination in this book, but getting there is work. Most likely you'll have to walk through several shallow riffles. If you persevere, you'll enjoy a pleasant meander through an evergreen forest to a grassy marsh with wide-open views. Solitude is almost guaranteed.

Getting to the river adds to the sense of remoteness: you'll need to drive for more than ten miles on a dirt road, keeping an eye out for an unmarked woods road that leads to an unmarked put-in. It's not easy to find, but if you follow the directions provided, you should do fine.

You reach the river by carrying a short distance along the woods road. From the put-in, you can travel downstream for 4.3 miles before coming to the first of several frothy rapids, the start of a long stretch navigable only by those with whitewater skills. This is the turnaround.

As soon as you put in, you enter a current that flows through a boulder garden. This is the most challenging water of the trip, but it lasts only a tenth of a mile. Experienced canoeists should be able to maneuver their boats around the rocks. If you have doubts, line your canoe or choose another trip.

The boulder garden ends with shallow riffles. You may need to walk your boat to pass over them. Over the next half-mile, the river alternates

Alder Bed Flow on the Middle Branch of the Oswegatchie. Photo by Phil Brown

between similar riffles and deeper flatwater. If the river is high enough, you can float over many of the shallows, but be prepared to get out of your boat when necessary. You also can expect to scrape bottom on occasion. Given these circumstances, this is a trip best undertaken in a durable canoe in spring or after a good rain.

At 1.25 miles from the put-in, you arrive at an island in the stream, with some riffles on the left (best avoided on the return trip). At 2.0 miles, just after passing a large boulder, the river leaves the forest for an attractive plain of shrubs and grasses. Within a mile, you enter a low marsh with views of Alder Bed Mountain to the west.

The scenic marsh extends for more than a mile, a rich habitat for waterfowl, trout, and deer. Because you're surrounded by low-growing grasses, you enjoy an expansive vista of the marsh and the whale-humped hills that enclose it. Other places in this book may lay claim to more dramatic scenery, but few can match the natural serenity of Alder Bed Flow.

At 4.1 miles, you leave the marsh and enter a narrow wooded channel,

Mallard Photo by Larry Master

which soon leads to the first rapid, just past the ruins of an old bridge. From the head of this short rapid, you can see more flatwater ahead, but don't be fooled: around the corner are longer, more difficult rapids.

On the return trip, you'll need to walk your boat up many of the shallows. In some places, you can line it from the shore, but you may find it easier to walk in the river. A good pair of water shoes is recommended.

DIRECTIONS: From NY 812 in Croghan, turn east on Belfort Road and drive 3.7 miles to Long Pond Road in Belfort. Turn right at this T-intersection and go 2.1 miles to an informational kiosk, where Long Pond Road makes a 90-degree turn to the left. Make the turn and continue on Long Pond Road for 8.2 miles to a large clearing. The dirt road beyond the clearing is known as Bear Cub Road or the Watson's East Main Haul Road. Follow it for another 9.8 miles to an old woods road on the left. This is the start of the portage. The road is unmarked and hard to spot, but you'll know you've gone a bit too far if you reach High Landing, a crest on the haul road with a view down a steep embankment to the river. The woods road is only 0.1 miles before High Landing. The carry to the put-in is about 500 feet.

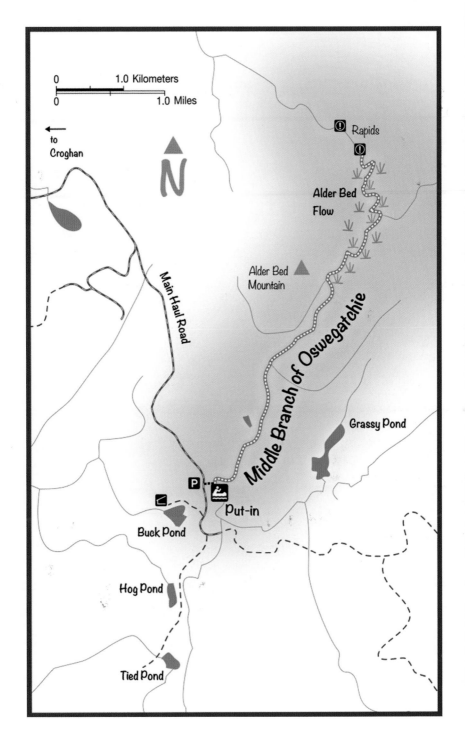

Riffles ahead on the Little River. Photo by Phil Brown

41. Little River

Length: 8 miles round-trip
Carries: Less than 0.1 miles
Shuttle: No
Motors: Permitted
Meander quotient: 28%
Put-in: 44°08.578' N, 75°06.655' W
National Geographic map: Old Forge/Oswegatchie

The Little River is well named: it's little known, little visited, and just plain little. But paddlers who dismiss it make a big mistake. This tributary of the Oswegatchie offers quiet and solitude in an unspoiled setting.

From Aldrich, a small colony of hunting camps, you can paddle up to four miles upstream before coming to impassable rapids. To get that far, you'll need to fight the current occasionally and carry over a few beaver dams and fallen trees, but that's a small price to pay for the enjoyment of a wild, serene stretch of river.

It's also possible to start at Route 3 east of Star Lake for a twelve-mile downstream cruise to Aldrich, but you must be prepared to scoot or carry over more than a dozen beaver dams in the three and a half miles between the put-in and Youngs Road, where the river flows through a culvert. You can avoid the concatenation of dams by putting in at Youngs Road, but you still will have to portage around a small whitewater gorge. Given these obstacles and the necessity of a shuttle, many paddlers will prefer the round-trip from Aldrich.

From the parking area, it's only a few hundred feet to the put-in near a boulder embedded with an iron ring, an artifact from the days when logs were floated down the river. Paddling upstream, you soon reach a large beaver dam. You can get around it by pulling out on the grassy bank on the left. A few miles farther upstream, the river may be blocked by a pair of log-jams. Unless a fellow paddler or a storm has cut through the debris, you'll need to exit your boat to get around the mess.

As you meander upriver, keep your eyes and ears open for geese, ducks,

The Little between Route 3 and Youngs Road. Photo by Pat Hendrick

ruffed grouse, red-winged blackbirds, pileated woodpeckers, white-throated sparrows, and hermit thrushes, to name just a few of the birds that dwell along the Little. You may also see a hawk circling above and wildlife tracks in the mudflats.

At the start of the trip, alder swamp dominates the landscape, but farther on the environs become more forested, with beautiful evergreen spires lining the banks. After three miles or so, you occasionally encounter shoals or short riffles. If the water is high, you should be able to paddle up most of these. In a few places, you may want to line your boat for brief stretches. At four miles, you reach longer, more serious rapids, and this is as far as most people will want to go. Turn around and enjoy the easy trip downstream.

DIRECTIONS: From the intersection of NY 3 and Youngs Road in Star Lake, drive west on NY 3 for three miles to Mill Road on the left, reached just before the highway crosses the Little River. Turn left and go 0.3 miles to a T-intersection. Turn left and go 0.6 miles to Coffin Mills Road. Turn right and go 3.5 miles to an access road on the left for the Aldrich Pond Wild Forest (reached shortly after crossing the Little in the hunting-camp community of Aldrich). Go down the access road 0.4 miles to Campsite 1 on the left. The short carry trail begins at the site.

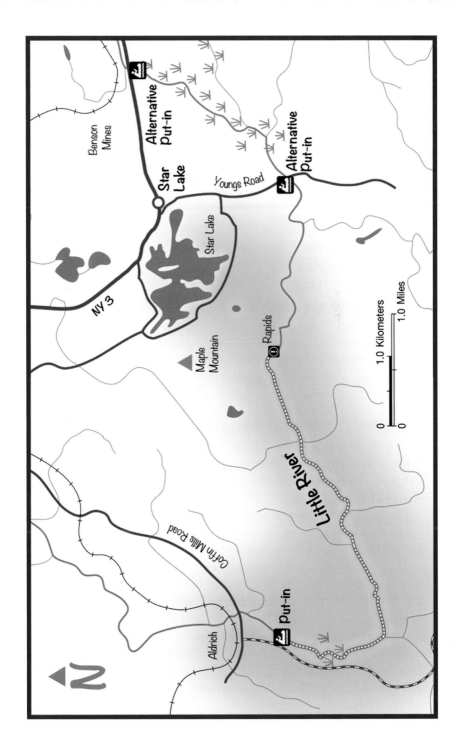

42. Oswegatchie River to High Falls

Length: Up to 23 miles round-trip
Carries: None
Shuttle: None
Motors: Prohibited
WSR status: Wild
Meander quotient: 45%
Put-in: 44°07.474' N, 74°57.610' W
National Geographic map: Old Forge/Oswegatchie

You can't see everything in the British Museum in a day. Nor should you expect to see in a single day all that the Oswegatchie River has to offer. That said, even a few hours in the British Museum is time well spent. You will be richer for having seen just the Elgin Marbles. Likewise, you won't forget a good day on the Oswegatchie.

High Falls is a popular destination for overnight excursions, but the round-trip of twenty-three miles is too ambitious for most day-trippers—especially if they want to relax and enjoy the sights. Two reasonable goals are High Rock (seven-mile round-trip) and the Buck Brook lean-to (thirteen-mile round-trip).

For those who do intend to stay the night, there are a few dozen campsites on the way to High Falls and even more farther upriver. Most of the best will likely be occupied on busy weekends.

The put-in is near a grassy clearing called Inlet, once the site of a hotel. Below here, the Oswegatchie flows through rapids to Wanakena a few miles away. Heading upstream, you encounter only flatwater, with a strong current in only a few places. The trip takes you though the Five Ponds Wilderness, a vast tract of Forest Preserve whose natural assets, besides the Oswegatchie, include the largest stand of old-growth forest in the Northeast and dozens of pristine ponds. It's good birding country. Just about every Adirondack bird can be found in the Wilderness Area, including boreal species such as the gray jay and black-backed woodpecker.

Most of time the Oswegatchie meanders through alder swamps or

The mouth of Buck Brook. Photo by Phil Brown

marshes, though it sometimes pulls alongside the forest. Before reaching High Rock, you pass through a corridor of evergreens that the guides of yesteryear dubbed Straight of the Woods. At 3.2 miles, you can spy High Rock rising above the watery plain, and in another quarter-mile you're there. Whether you're going on or not, take a few minutes to take in the scenery from this overlook. There is a good landing in the little cove just beyond the rock, with a path leading to a campsite and the twenty-foot summit.

High Rock affords a bird's-eye view of what hitherto you have experienced only from the water: endless wetlands and the serpentine curves of a river hell-bent on finding the longest distance between two points. You may be joined by hikers: a foot trail from Wanakena passes by High Rock.

A mile and a half beyond High Rock, you come to the lean-to near Griffin Rapids. Often canoeists won't notice the rapids at all, but when the water level is low, there are exposed rocks. In another mile and a half, you arrive at the lean-to at the mouth of Buck Brook. Although you can paddle only a short way up the brook, the little stream affords an impressive vista of

The serpentine Oswegatchie River. Photo by Carl Heilman II

grassy marshes with low hills on the horizon. It's one of the prettiest scenes you'll find between Inlet and High Falls.

You enjoy essentially the same view from the lean-to. Shaded by tall pines, the log edifice is an ideal lunch spot. It even has a picnic table. The lean-to is 6.4 miles from Inlet. If you turn around here, you'll have had a full day. For those who want to continue, here are a few notes:

• 8.0 miles: the river pulls beside the Wanakena hiking trail on the left.

• 9.4 miles: you pass under a footbridge. This trail leads through the aforementioned old growth en route to Big Shallow Pond. The current under the bridge is swift.

• 11.5 miles: High Falls. The falls are powerful, though the drop is only fifteen feet. As Paul Jamieson observed, "Since this is about half of the total drop between the head of the fall and Inlet, perhaps the name is justified."

If camping, you can spend a day exploring the Oswegatchie above High Falls, but be prepared to pull over a large number of beaver dams. This part of the river is better done from the other direction on the Oswegatchie Traverse. For details on this option, see the appendix on multiday trips.

DIRECTIONS: From the Oswegatchie River bridge in Cranberry Lake, drive west on NY 3 for 9.9 miles to Sunny Lake Road on the left. As soon as you make the turn, turn left onto a dirt lane known as Inlet Road. Follow it 3.2 miles to a grassy parking area at the end. If coming from Star Lake, Sunny Lake Road is reached 3.2 miles east of the intersection of NY3 and Youngs Road.

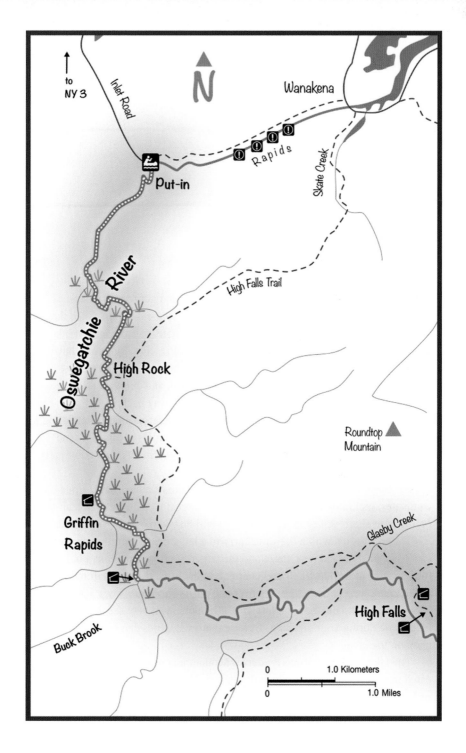

to
NY 3

Inlet Road

Wanakena

N

Put-in

Rapids

Skate Creek

High Falls Trail

River

Oswegatchie

High Rock

Roundtop
Mountain

Griffin
Rapids

Glasby Creek

High Falls

Buck Brook

0   1.0 Kilometers

0   1.0 Miles

43. Lake Lila

....

Length: 8 to13 miles
Carries: 0.3 miles to put-in
Shuttle: No
Motors: Prohibited
Put-in: 44°01.1161' N, 74°43.8007' W
National Geographic map: Old Forge/Oswegatchie

With its sandy beaches, pine-studded islands, and gorgeous sunsets, Lake Lila has been a favorite destination of canoe-campers since the state purchased the lake in 1978. At nearly 1,500 acres, it's the largest lake in the Adirondacks surrounded entirely by Forest Preserve. You don't have to spend the night, though. Day-trippers can see the best of Lila by paddling across the lake, hiking up Frederica Mountain, and exploring Shingle Shanty Brook and perhaps the Beaver River on the way back.

It will be a long but rewarding day, with up to thirteen miles of paddling and three miles of hiking. You can reduce the water miles to eight or nine by just poking your nose into the Beaver and Shingle Shanty instead of paddling all the way to private land.

For those who do want to spend the night, Lake Lila has twenty-four campsites, including one on each of the four largest islands and one lean-to on the west shore. All or most of the sites will be taken on busy weekends.

The trip begins with a 0.3-mile carry to a large beach from which you can see a small island near shore and the larger Snell Island about a half-mile away. Paddle past Snell and continue in the same direction all the way to the lake's west shore, 2.5 miles from the put-in. En route, keep Spruce Island and Buck Island on the left. If you're lucky, you may see an osprey or bald eagle during your crossing. Beware that west winds can create a nasty chop on the lake.

The takeout for climbing Frederica Mountain is near Campsite 9, located in a clearing north of Mosquito Island. The clearing was once the site of Forest Lodge, a rustic palace built by William Seward Webb, a wealthy entrepreneur who bought the lake in the late 1800s and named it after his

Sandy shoreline at Lake Lila. Photo by Ray Palmer

wife, Lila Osgood Vanderbilt. Before then, it was called Smith's Lake after a hermit who lived on its shores. Webb named Frederica Mountain—once known as Smith's Rock or Pratt's Mountain—after his daughter. The state tore down the lodge in 1984.

Walk through the clearing to a dirt road (closed to vehicles, except those used to reach inholdings). Turn right and continue a tenth of a mile to an intersection with another dirt road. Turn left and walk 0.8 miles to a trail on the right (0.3 miles after crossing railroad tracks). From the road it's a gentle 0.6-mile climb to Frederica's ledges, which offer views across the lake of numerous mountains, including some of the High Peaks in the east. "The eye rests upon a scene more striking and beautiful than that surveyed from many loftier elevations," the nineteenth-century writer Edwin R. Wallace noted in his *Descriptive Guide to the Adirondacks.* That's as true today.

After returning to the lake, paddle south along the shore. In a short distance, you come to the start of the Beaver River, which is quite wide. You can travel a mile down the outlet before reaching private property. To reach Shingle Shanty Brook, the lake's major inlet, paddle around Buck Island and

Frederica Mountain's view of Lila. Photo by Susan Bibeau

cross a large bay to the stream's mouth on the bay's east shore.

Shingle Shanty is an enchanting stream that twists for miles through a huge wetland. It also is a link in the Lila Traverse, a pond-hopping trip that begins on Little Tupper Lake. From Lila, you can go up Shingle Shanty for more than 1.5 miles before reaching private land. A carry trail starts at the private-land boundary and leads in 0.75 miles to Lilypad Pond.

Among the wildflowers you might see on the brook are gentian, turtle-head, arrowhead, and cardinal flower. It's also good habitat for birds, including some of the boreal species. Upon returning to the lake, follow the bay's north shore and then angle northeast back toward Snell Island and the put-in.

DIRECTIONS: From Tupper Lake, drive south on NY 30 for 9.5 miles after crossing the Raquette River and turn right onto Sabattis Circle Road. Go 3.1 miles to a three-way intersection. Bear right onto County 10 (Sabattis Road) and go 2.2 miles to a dirt road marked by a Lake Lila sign. Turn left and go 2.4 miles to the parking area. If coming from Long Lake hamlet, drive north for 6.4 miles after crossing Long Lake and turn left onto Sabattis Road. Follow this road to the three-way intersection and then turn left and proceed as described. The carry trail begins on the south side of the parking area. Note: the access road may be gated in mud season.

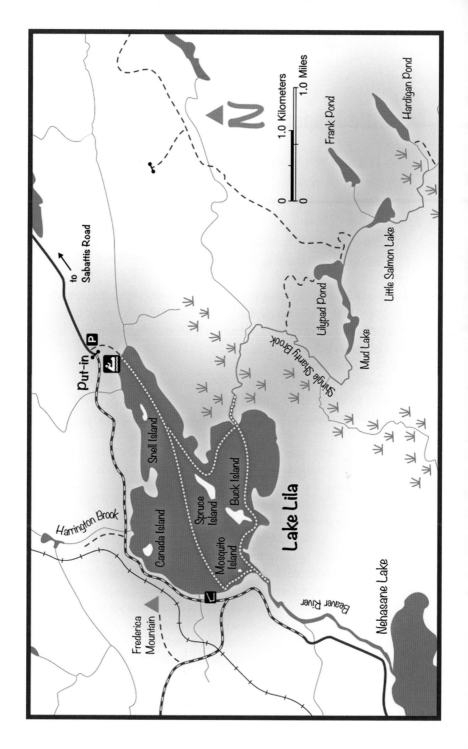

N

1.0 Kilometers

1.0 Miles

0

0

Frank Pond

Hardigan Pond

to Sabattis Road

Little Salmon Lake

Lilypad Pond

Shingle Shanty Brook

Mud Lake

Put-in

P

Snell Island

Buck Island

Spruce Island

Canada Island

Mosquito Island

Harrington Brook

Lake Lila

Frederica Mountain

Beaver River

Nehasane Lake

44. Little Tupper Lake to Rock Pond

Length: 13 miles round-trip
Carries: 150 yards
Shuttle: No
Motors: Prohibited
Put-in: 44°03.121' N, 74°35.157' W
National Geographic map: Old Forge/Oswegatchie

Governor George Pataki made headlines in 1997 when he announced the state would buy Little Tupper Lake, the largest privately owned lake in the Northeast. Pataki went on to preserve a million acres in New York State during his time in office, but the Little Tupper tract remains one of the treasures of his conservation legacy.

Altogether, the state purchased 14,700 acres from the Whitney family in that deal. Besides Little Tupper, the property included Rock Pond and a number of smaller ponds.

If you have two or three days, the best way to appreciate the tract's watery riches is to take a canoe trip from Little Tupper to Lake Lila—a journey that entails paddling on two large lakes, four backcountry ponds, and three enchanting streams. If you have only a day, though, you won't be disappointed in a trip to Rock Pond and back.

The Whitneys constructed several buildings on the north shore of Little Tupper to serve as headquarters for their lumbering operations. The complex now is the state's headquarters for the William C. Whitney Wilderness. Besides these buildings and two homes, you won't see any development on Little Tupper's twenty miles of shoreline.

The headquarters is the starting point of your trip. The put-in is a sandy beach next to a boathouse. One of the private homes lies across the lake. As you pull out onto the water, you can see Buck Mountain and its fire tower to the east. Your objective lies in the other direction: the outlet of Rock Pond at the southwest end of Little Tupper.

Rounding a piney point, you soon see the other home on the north shore. After a half-mile of paddling, you've left civilization behind. In a mile, you

Returning to Little Tupper on the Rock Pond outlet. Photo by Phil Brown

come to the first of several islands along your route, some thickly wooded, some nothing more than barren rocks.

Little Tupper is a shallow lake whose surface is often whipped by west winds. On a breezy day, you may be fighting whitecaps during the 4.5-mile paddle to the Rock Pond outlet. If so, keep close to the shore for shelter and safety.

Hugging the shore has another advantage: it gives you the opportunity to listen for the many species of wood warblers that dwell among the hardwoods and tall pines. Birds that might be observed on the water or in the shallows include common loons, great blue herons, and various ducks. Bald eagles sometimes fly over the lake.

The greatest rarity is to be found not in the air but in the water: the Little Tupper brook trout. This ancient strain has survived in Little Tupper and Rock Pond since the last glacier retreated, some twelve thousand years ago. Unfortunately, some yahoo illegally introduced bass into the lake after the state purchased it. The non-native fish threaten to crowd out the heritage trout. The good news is that Little Tupper trout are faring well in backcountry ponds where they have been introduced by state biologists.

About four miles from the put-in, you arrive at Short Island, the largest island in Little Tupper. From here, you can see a large wetland on the lake's northwest shore. If you have time at the end of the day, it can be explored by paddling up the Charley Pond outlet.

To reach the Rock Pond outlet, aim for a small island with a few pines that sits near the mouth. At the outset, the stream is quite broad, its surface adorned with pickerelweed and pond lilies. Leatherleaf, buttonbush, and other wetland shrubs line the shores. You also can find carnivorous pitcher plants and sundews. Birders should keep an eye out for boreal birds along the stream.

The stream's most conspicuous denizen is the beaver. You'll pass more than a half-dozen lodges and go over at least three dams en route to Rock Pond.

A mile from Little Tupper, you come to a fork in the stream, with a campsite on the left. The right fork is the outlet of Bum Pond. Bear left to continue to Rock Pond. In another quarter-mile, you reach the biggest beaver dam on the stream. Most likely, you'll have to get out of your boat and pull it over. A little beyond, look for the carry trail on the left, about a mile and a half from the lake.

The short portage around rapids leads to a bridge on an old logging road. Put in here and follow the wide channel a quarter-mile or so to the pond. You've now traveled 1.8 miles from the lake and, barring detours, 6.4 miles from Whitney headquarters.

At 285 acres, Rock Pond qualifies as a lake, but whatever you call it, it's a beautiful sheet of water. Salmon Lake Mountain to the south dominates the backdrop. This 2,500-foot peak, which has a fire tower, is on land still owned by the Whitney family. You can stop for lunch at one of the five shoreline campsites or on the big island in the middle of the pond.

If you're up for more paddling, head for the inlet at the pond's southeast corner, keeping left of the island. Once on the stream, you'll have to cross a few beaver dams, but your reward will be solitude and tranquility in an absolutely wild setting. You can go about a half-mile before reaching the private-land boundary (which is not posted). If you do go this far, your round-trip will be about sixteen miles—more than enough to give you a taste of the Whitney Wilderness.

On the return trip, you'll enjoy a final treat while paddling down Little Tupper Lake: views straight ahead of Mount Morris (another fire-tower summit) and the Seward Range (in the High Peaks Wilderness). And chances are you'll have the west wind at your back.

DIRECTIONS: From Tupper Lake, drive south on NY 30 for 9.5 miles after crossing the Raquette River and turn right onto Sabattis Circle Road. Go 3.1 miles to a three-way intersection. Bear right onto County 10 (Sabattis Road) and go 1.3 miles to the access road for the Whitney Wilderness headquarters. Turn left and go 0.3 miles to the parking lot. If coming from Long Lake hamlet, drive north for 6.4 miles after crossing Long Lake and turn left onto Sabattis Road. Follow this road to the three-way intersection and then the headquarters.

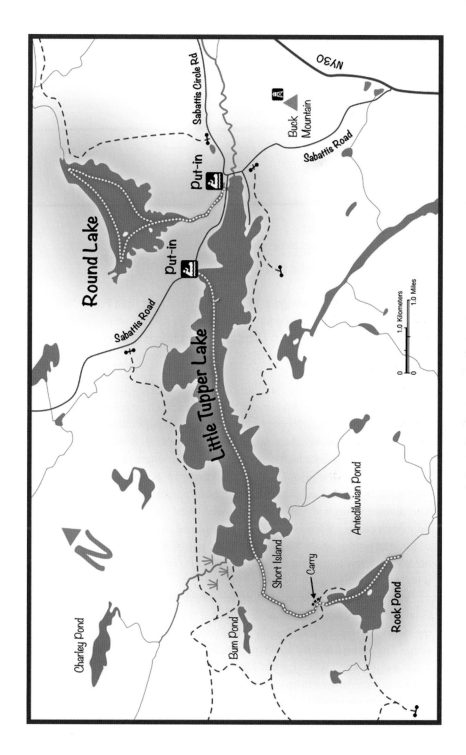

Round Lake

NY30

Sabattis Circle Rd

Buck Mountain

Sabattis Road

Put-in

Put-in

Sabattis Road

Little Tupper Lake

Charley Pond

Bum Pond

Short Island

Carry

Antediluvian Pond

Rock Pond

1.0 Kilometers

1.0 Miles

N

45. Round Lake

....

Length: 7 to 8 miles
Carries: None
Shuttle: No
Motors: Prohibited
Put-in: 44°03.300' N, 74°33.721' W
National Geographic map: Old Forge/Oswegatchie.

One way to see the Adirondack Park is to climb all the High Peaks, but you'd get a more well-rounded picture of the region by visiting all the ponds and lakes named Round. There are at least fifteen of them scattered about the Park. You'd do well to start with the Round Lake near Little Tupper Lake.

Acquired by the state in 2005, this four-hundred-acre jewel is the centerpiece of the Round Lake Wilderness. You can reach it by a mile-long paddle from the put-in on Little Tupper (whose outlet is Round's inlet), but it's easier to start at Round Lake's own put-in along Sabattis Road.

You launch in a little backwater near the bridge where the Little Tupper outlet flows under the road. The broad, flat stream is bordered by a large wetland that contains sedge meadows, spruce-fir swamps, and boreal bogs. The channel teems with pickerelweed, water lilies, and other aquatic vegetation. After passing a few beaver lodges, you come to a rock islet at the head of the lake proper, about 0.9 miles from the put-in. You can make a circuit of the lake in a few hours, but you may want to get out of your boat to explore a few places.

Two points of interest are the wooded islands situated some distance from the south shore. Rocks line the shore of the first, located about a quarter-mile from the islet, but there is a good takeout on the southwest shore. The second, located another 0.4 miles away, is the more interesting. It has a piney knoll with views of Mount Morris and nearby Buck Mountain (which are also visible from the lake). Take out on the northwest side of the island. From the second island, you can paddle west to a boggy inlet at the end of the large bay.

Round Lake. Photo by Phil Brown

Eventually, you'll want to make your way to the outlet at the lake's north end. Shortly before reaching it, you come to two bedrock islands, fine places for lolling in the sun on a warm day. At the foot of the lake, a much bigger island splits the outlet in two. There is a spillway on the left channel.

Round Lake Stream, as the outlet is called, is a pretty waterway with a number of cascades. If you want to see some of its scenery, you can hike along a trail that parallels the stream. From the spillway, paddle up the east shore a quarter-mile to a small beach with a rivulet running through it. Follow a trail from the beach to an old woods road, then turn left and follow the road a short distance to a concrete dam. After the dam, the unmarked trail (used as a carry by those heading to the Bog River) gets rougher.

Although you can see Round Lake in an afternoon, you might want to spend the night, staying at one of the eleven campsites that ring the lake. One of the best is on a rise near the beach.

DIRECTIONS: From Tupper Lake, drive south on NY 30 for 9.5 miles after crossing the Raquette River and turn right onto Sabattis Circle Road. Go 3.1 miles to a three-way intersection. As soon as you turn right, you come to the Round Lake parking area. The put-in is about 100 yards farther up the road on the right. If coming from Long Lake hamlet, drive north for 6.4 miles on NY 30 after crossing Long Lake and turn left onto Sabattis Road. Follow this road to the three-way intersection and the parking lot.

46. Bog River & Hitchins Pond

Length: 6 miles round-trip
Carries: None
Shuttle: No
Motors: Prohibited
Meander quotient: 34%
Put-in: 44°06.958' N, 74°37.584' W
National Geographic map: Old Forge/Oswegatchie

In the late 1800s, the entrepreneur Abbot Augustus Low acquired nearly forty-six thousand acres in the Bog River basin and created a thriving business in the wilderness, selling timber, maple syrup, bottled water, and wildberry jams. Although a forest fire in 1908 ruined Low's enterprise, paddlers continue to benefit from his industriousness.

Low built a dam on the Bog River in 1903 to generate electricity for his Horse Shoe Forestry Company. Known today as Lows Lower Dam, it backs up the Bog as far as Hitchins Pond, creating a three-mile still-water.

For a pleasant day trip, it's hard to beat the leisurely paddle up the river from the dam to the pond, followed by a short hike to a scenic overlook on Lows Ridge. The dam is also the starting point for longer canoe treks to Lows Lake, the Oswegatchie River, and Lake Lila. On weekends in peak season, the small parking area is often full.

As a wilder alternative, you can put in at the Horseshoe Lake outlet and follow it to the Bog River. This is not for everyone, as paddlers on the tiny stream must contend with beaver dams and encroaching alders. But it can be done if water levels are high enough. The surveyor Verplanck Colvin reached the Bog via this route in 1873, long before A.A. Low built his dam. If you do start here, consider leaving a bicycle at the dam and pedaling back to your car. That way, you won't have to paddle up the outlet on the return and you'll get to see more of the Bog River.

Near the Lower Dam, the Bog resembles a large pool. As you paddle upstream, the river corridor soon narrows. Stumps in the water serve as

Hitchins Pond and the Bog River as seen from Lows Ridge.   Photo by Phil Brown

occasional reminders that the land has been flooded. At 0.6 miles, you pass a piney point on the right and enter a broad pool. Angle right toward a big rock that slopes into the water. As you approach the rock, look for the river's weedy channel on the right.

You reach the mouth of the Horseshoe Lake outlet at 1.2 miles and soon after pass under a railroad trestle. The wide channel offers views of Lows Ridge and the cliffs on Silver Lake Mountain. After skirting a grassy marsh, you come to Hitchins Pond at 2.25 miles.

Common loons nest on Hitchins, and bald eagles sometimes hunt there. Indeed, this whole trip is good for birding. Among the other birds that may be seen are gray jay, boreal chickadee, and a number of species of wood warblers and ducks, according to the guidebook *Adirondack Birding*.

When you reach the pond, turn left and head for the southwest end, where there is an obvious landing. Now that you've paddled nearly three miles, it's time to stretch your legs. A short path paralleling the Bog River leads past stone foundations to Lows Upper Dam (which impounds the nine-mile-long Lows Lake). From the dam, walk to the right toward other stone foundations and look for a trail register.

Black-backed woodpecker Photo by Larry Master

The sign says the trail is 1.1 miles, but it's actually less than a mile. It switchbacks up the ridge and emerges from the woods onto a rocky spine with a spectacular view of the Bog River winding through wetlands. In the distance you can discern many of the High Peaks, including Whiteface Mountain, Santanoni Peak, Algonquin Peak, and Mount Marcy. A plaque on the ridge memorializes Low's son, also named Abbot Augustus.

On the return paddle, you may want to poke around the vast wetlands bordering Hitchins Pond to the north and southeast. It's thought that these marshes and bogs serve as a habitat corridor connecting the Massawepie Mire to the northwest and the Round Lake wetlands to the southeast. They may be visited by northern birds like the black-backed woodpecker, palm warbler, and boreal chickadee. Horseshoe Lake's outlet is also worth exploring on the way back, but you'll likely have to pull over a beaver dam or two to get very far.

If you want to extend your outing, you can paddle part way up Lows Lake. The lake resembles a wide river at first. The main lake comes into view at the far end of Gooseneck Island. If you do a loop around the island, you add more than nine miles to the round-trip—for fifteen miles total. A less-strenuous alternative is to paddle the flatwater above Bog River Falls, which you passed on your drive to the lower dam. You can go nearly two miles before reaching rapids near the confluence with Round Lake's outlet. A short path leads from the falls parking to a put-in.

DIRECTIONS: From Tupper Lake village, drive south on NY 30. Seven miles after crossing the Raquette River, turn right onto NY 421. (You soon pass Bog River Falls, where the Bog flows into Tupper Lake.) Go 5.9 miles to the Lower Dam access road. Turn left and go 0.7 miles to the parking area at the end. Put in near the dam. To put in the Horseshoe Lake outlet, continue on 421 instead of turning onto the access road. The bridge over the outlet is 0.4 miles past the turn. Park along the road. If coming from the south, NY 421 is reached 13.0 miles from the bridge over Long Lake.

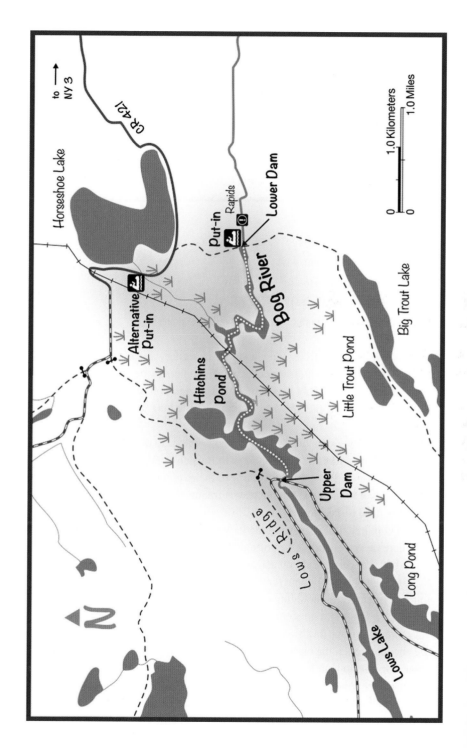

to NY 3

CR 421

Horseshoe Lake

Put-in

Rapids

Lower Dam

Bog River

Alternative Put-in

Hitchins Pond

Little Trout Pond

Big Trout Lake

Upper Dam

Low's Ridge

Long Pond

Low's Lake

N

1.0 Kilometers
1.0 Miles

47. Grass River Flow & Massawepie Mire

Length: 10-mile through trip
Carries: At least 4 totaling about 0.3 miles
Shuttle: 14.6 miles
Motors: Permitted
WSR status: Scenic
Meander quotient: 44%
Put-in: 44°12.838' N, 74°40.122' W
Takeout: 44°15.298' N, 74°45.291' W
National Geographic map: Old Forge/Oswegatchie

Although the Grass River Flow abounds in scenery and birdlife, the difficulty of reaching it discourages many paddlers from going there. So you can add solitude to its list of attractions. An impoundment of the South Branch of the Grass, the flow is only about a mile long, but you can paddle upriver beyond it for miles.

There are two ways of reaching the flow. One is to do a round-trip from Route 3. This requires a 0.1-mile carry to Balsam Pond, a paddle across the small pond, and another 0.1-mile carry to the river. From the put-in, it's only a mile upriver to the flow, but the way is frequently blocked by blowdown. You may need to exit your boat a half-dozen times. If you go this route, you should continue upriver beyond the flow to explore the Massawepie Mire and increase your padding-to-portaging ratio.

A better excursion, if you can arrange a shuttle, is to start farther up the Grass and paddle downriver, ending the trip at Route 3. The one-way journey is ten miles, including carries. The through trip begins at a small bridge on a logging road south of the Massawepie Boy Scout Camp. At the start, the river is narrow, twisty, and often shallow. Numerous beaver dams are encountered in the eight miles to the flow, but if the water is high, you should be able to paddle over most.

The river winds through the Massawepie Mire, one of the largest wetland complexes in the Adirondacks. The mire harbors a number of species of boreal birds, including the rare spruce grouse. Other species of note in-

Burnt Rock on the Grass River. Photo by Mike Lynch

clude gray jay, palm warbler, Lincoln's sparrow, black-backed woodpecker, rusty blackbird, and boreal chickadee.

Although the setting is mostly wild, there are a few signs of development: the Grasse River Club at 1.0 mile, a steel footbridge at 1.6 miles, an old railroad bridge at 3.0 miles, and a logging road bridge at 5.3 miles. Also, there is one camp on the flow.

At 4.2 miles, you come to a natural landmark: Burnt Rock, a twenty-five-foot cliff that rises straight out of the water and overlooks the river plain. Unfortunately, the cliff is posted land. If you're doing a round-trip from Route 3, Burnt Rock is a good turnaround destination. From the highway, it's six miles, including carries.

From Burnt Rock, you have about four miles of downstream paddling to the Grass River Flow. As you near the flow, the alders start to thin out, giving way to grassy hummocks, which in turn give way to emergent grasses. Once you're out of the alders, you enjoy longer views, with nearby peaks visible. The flow is frequented by a number of waterfowl, such as Canada geese, common mergansers, great blue herons, and American bitterns. Biologists have identified the wetland on the north shore as a "poor fen," which is similar to a bog but richer in flora.

When you get to the end of the flow, pull out on the left and cross a

The foot of the Grass River Flow. Photo by Phil Brown

logging road. Shortly after putting in again, you'll encounter the first of the several blowdowns en route to the takeout. If you don't mind carrying, you can take out on the right and portage about a quarter-mile along the bank to bypass three blowdowns at once.

The start of the carry trail to Balsam Pond is marked by a yellow disk on the right bank. Soon after climbing the bank, you can see the pond to the left. Although the main trail continues straight, look for a path leading to the shore. Paddle straight across the pond to the takeout on the north shore. Another trail leads to the highway.

DIRECTIONS: From the village of Tupper Lake, drive west on NY 3. About 5.5 miles after crossing the Raquette River, note the turn for the Massawepie Boy Scouts Camp on the left. If you do a through trip, you'll return here for the put-in. For now, continue on NY 3 for 9.4 miles to the takeout, which is marked by a small "Canoe Access" sign that's hard to spot. When you get to Sevey Corners, where NY 3 meets NY 56, check your odometer. The takeout is 3.5 miles farther (on the left side of the road). Park along the shoulder. For the put-in, return to Massawepie. Turn right and follow the main dirt road through the camp for 4.8 miles to a four-way intersection. Turn right and go 0.4 miles to a parking area on the right (on the way, bear left at a Y intersection). The put-in bridge is about a hundred yards farther down the road.

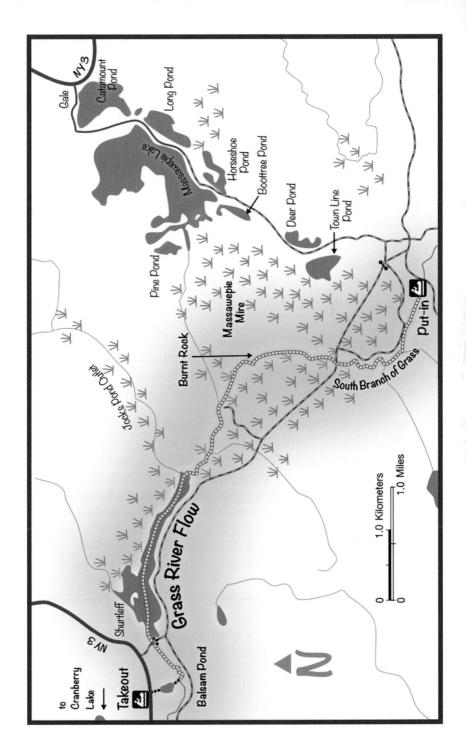

48. Jordan River

Length: 10 to 34 miles round-trip
Carries: 1.6 miles
Shuttle: No
Motors: Prohibited on river
WSR status: Scenic
Meander quotient: 52%
Put-in: 44°21.2070' N, 74°43.5120' W
National Geographic map: Saranac/Paul Smiths

Northern hardwood forests dominate the Adirondack Park, but in the northwest sector the landscape often resembles the subarctic taiga found in Canada: large swaths of evergreens, with lots of swamps and bogs. The region serves as a refuge for boreal plants and birds, including the spruce grouse, which is endangered in New York State.

To protect this habitat, the Adirondack Council has proposed that New York State establish a 73,300-acre Boreal Wilderness east of Carry Falls Reservoir. Flowing through the heart of this tract is the seldom-visited Jordan River. The land planner George Davis, who authored the wilderness proposal, wrote about canoeing the Jordan just after dawn: "Civilization could be hundreds of miles away as the mist rises from the leatherleaf-dominated fens, as the white-throated sparrow and the ruby-crowned kinglet call, while the towering old-growth pines drift in and out of the mist."

The state would not be able to create the Boreal Wilderness unless it acquired more land, but the Jordan is open to the public now. Getting there is not easy: you have to paddle 2.5 miles on Carry Falls Reservoir and carry 1.6 miles before putting in above the river's sole extended stretch of rapids. The difficulty of access has kept the Jordan wild and pristine. Indeed, DEC refuses even to create primitive tent sites along its banks. If you spend the night, you must camp at least 150 feet from the river.

The Jordan originates at Sunset Pond (also known as Marsh Pond) and flows eighteen miles to Carry Falls Reservoir, a huge hydropower impound-

Encountering a giant deadfall on the Jordon River. Photo by Mark Bowie

ment on the Raquette River. Because the headwaters are on private land (which is gated), paddlers must approach the river from the reservoir. The starting point is the Parmenter Campsite on the reservoir's southwest shore, where the power company runs a campground, picnic area, and boat launch. There is no charge for launching a boat.

At the put-in, the reservoir is about three hundred yards wide. Paddle to the opposite side and follow the shoreline north. You may see motorboats, especially in summer. At 2.1 miles, you reach the mouth of the Jordan and the camps of the Jordan Club, established in 1894. Do not go upriver here as you would soon encounter the rapids. Continue down the reservoir about a half-mile and look for a rusting old truck beside a sandy beach. The carry begins here. Apart from its length, the route is not difficult. It follows an old jeep trail that's suitable for a canoe cart. Soon after entering the woods, you pass a few other rusting vehicles and come to a fork. Bear right here and at all other forks farther down the trail. At 1.4 miles, you reach a well-maintained logging road. Turn right and go 0.2 miles to a bridge over the Jordan. Put in on the northeast side of the bridge.

Exploring a green corridor. Photo by Mark Bowie

How far can you go upriver? For day-trippers, an ambitious goal would be Bear Brook, reached about five miles from the put-in the bridge, or the Jordan Lake outlet, about a mile and a half farther on. The round-trip to Bear Brook entails more than fifteen miles of paddling and 3.2 miles of portaging. Add three miles of paddling if you go to the Jordan Lake outlet. Given these distances, no doubt many paddlers will choose to turn around short of Bear Brook.

Don't expect long views of distant peaks from the Jordan. The river is a world in itself. Heading upstream, you wind through corridors of white pine, spruce, and other evergreens. Even when you encounter alder thickets, the forest is usually close—though if you paddle beyond the Jordan Lake outlet, you will see more extensive wetlands.

DIRECTIONS: From the village of Tupper Lake, drive west on NY 3 to NY 56 at Sevey Corners (11.4 miles after crossing the Raquette River in Piercefield). Turn right and go 4.1 miles to the Parmenter Site on the right. Follow the access road to a parking lot and boat launch at south end of Carry Falls Reservoir.

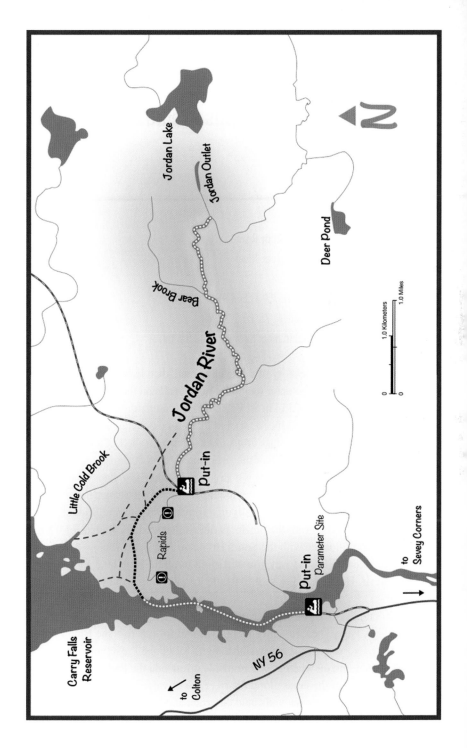

49. Grass River to Lampson Falls

Length: 9 miles

Carries: 0.5 miles

Shuttle: 1.8 miles (optional)

Motors: Permitted

WSR status: Scenic; Study River

WSR status: Scenic; Study River

Meander quotient: 46%

Put-in: 44°22.787' N, 75°03.864' W

Takeout: 44°24.300' N, 75°03.698' W

National Geographic map: Saranac/Paul Smiths

Paul Jamieson tells the story of a Frenchwoman, then living in the United States, who exclaimed upon seeing Lampson Falls on the Grass River, "There is nothing so beautiful in all France!" Her compatriots might disagree (Mount Blanc is nothing to sneeze at), but there is no denying the allure of this powerful cascade. The Grass drops forty feet over a shelf of ancient bedrock that extends the full width of the river, some 150 feet across.

Below the crashing whitewater is a large pool bordered by giant white pines. It's a great spot for picnicking, for swimming, or for ending a canoe trip.

The trip begins a few miles south on a tributary stream, the Middle Branch of the Grass. From the put-in, paddle down Middle Branch for 0.8 miles to the confluence with the South Branch of the Grass (below here, it is the Main Branch). On the way you will wind through shrub land and floodplain forests. Be prepared to deal with a few beaver dams and perhaps some blowdown.

Incidentally, by the time you reach the main stem you will have left the Adirondack Park. The Grass meanders back and forth across the Blue Line a few times, so you may see occasional signs for Forest Preserve or State Forest, depending on whether you're inside or outside the Park. Bear in mind that some of the lands along the river are private.

Once on the larger river, you could turn right and head downstream to Lampson Falls. This would mean a one-way trip of only four miles or so, not in-

Lampson Falls on the Grass River.   Photo by Ray Palmer

cluding the carry at the end. You could do a round-trip instead, but you'd have to contend with a mild current (it's strongest on the Middle Branch) on the return. Another option is to extend the outing by paddling upriver on the Grass. You can go a little more than two miles before turning around at some rapids. Altogether, this gives you eight or nine miles of paddling, enough to justify a bike shuttle. It's a quick and easy ride on a rural road back to the put-in. If you do a shuttle, however, you must carry or wheel your boat a half-mile from the takeout to the highway.

If you opt to head upriver on the Grass, you'll find the current is usually gentle. Silver maples grow in the floodplains. About a mile from the confluence, you come to a house with a mowed lawn that stands in stark contrast to the wild landscape. A little beyond, you pass a large sandy bank, perhaps an esker, topped by pines and hemlocks. After 2.1 miles of paddling upstream, you'll see another house beside the rapids. This is the place to turn around.

The downstream cruise goes quickly. You should make it back to the confluence in forty-five minutes, give or take ten minutes. As you continue downriver, you wind through marshes and alder swamps, with occasional views of nearby hills. Except for a few small homes, the river corridor is wild. You may want to explore some of the bays and side channels, which are good habitat for ducks.

About two miles from the confluence, a rocky cliff rises above the river—a surprising sight after you've spent hours meandering through flat-

The Main Branch of the Grass. Photo by Phil Brown

lands. Farther on you may notice bedrock slabs in the woods on the left.

You can hear the falls well before reaching them. Just before the takeout there is a large bay on the right that's worth exploring. It leads to a smaller bay. It's possible to do a loop and re-enter the main channel upstream of the bay's mouth.

Just beyond the bay, a rocky point on the right bank slopes into the water. In the still water on the upstream side of the point, look for a flat landing among the alders. Take out here and follow a rough path fifteen feet to an obvious trail, then take the trail a short distance to the woods road leading to Lampson Falls. Leave your boat here and turn left to visit the falls. There are numerous paths leading to the cascade and the pool below. Be careful not to slip on the wet rock.

After you've taken it all in, return to your boat and follow the road (which is closed to vehicles) about 0.4 miles to the highway. The entire carry from the river is about a half mile. The trail and road are suitable for a canoe cart.

DIRECTIONS: From NY 3 just west of Cranberry Lake, turn north onto Tooley Pond Road (near the Oswegatchie River). Drive 17.1 miles to County 27 and turn right. You will cross the North Branch of the Grass in 2 miles and reach the parking area for the Lampson Falls takeout in 4.1 miles. You can leave a bike or car here for a shuttle. To reach the put-in, head back on County 27 for 1.8 miles to a grassy road on the right marked by a wooden "Canoe Access" sign. The road soon leads to a parking area. A grassy path leads to the North Branch.

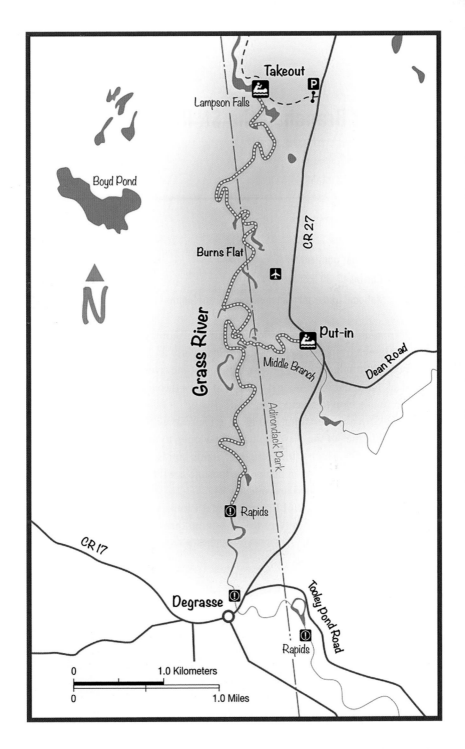

Takeout

Lampson Falls

Boyd Pond

CR 27

Burns Flat

N

Grass River

Put-in

Middle Branch

Dean Road

Adirondack Park

Rapids

CR 17

Degrasse

Tooley Pond Road

Rapids

0   1.0 Kilometers

0   1.0 Miles

50. West Branch of the St. Regis

Length: 7 miles round-trip
Carries: 2 totaling 0.4 miles
Shuttle: No
Motors: Permitted
WSR status: Scenic
Meander quotient: 38%
Put-in: 44°30.559' N, 74°41.016' W
National Geographic map: Saranac/Paul Smiths

In *Adirondack Canoe Waters: North Flow*, Paul Jamieson describes the West Branch of the St. Regis as the "most tightly locked-up river of the northern Adirondacks." The first forty miles of the river lie within the Adirondack Park, but only the first mile or so flows through public land—and that section is hard to reach.

Thanks to a conservation-easement agreement with a timber company, about eight miles of the West Branch is now open to the public from May 1 to September 30. Much of this length contains rapids, but flatwater paddlers can enjoy a 3.5-mile stretch that winds through a wild and scenic floodplain, great habitat for waterfowl and other birds.

The state Department of Environmental Conservation has created four parking areas on the Main Haul Road running through the timber company's property. Near each lot is a trail leading to the river. The best flatwater paddling is between the second and third put-ins. Theoretically, you could do a downstream float from the third to the second put-in, but this requires a long, nasty portage along overgrown,

Great blue heron Photo by Larry Master

A rare paddler on the West Branch of the St. Regis.   Photo by Phil Brown

slash-strewn logging roads. By opting for a round-trip, you avoid this unpleasantness and get to spend twice as much time on the water. You are likely to have the river to yourself.

The round-trip from the second designated put-in begins with a portage of less than a tenth of a mile around rapids to bedrock outcrops along the shore. As you head upriver, you are treated to views of waving marsh grasses and wooded hills. At 0.4 miles, you pass a log cabin on the right, which belongs to a hunting club that leases land from the timber company. The current is hardly noticeable as the broad river winds through marsh and past sandy banks topped by tall pines. Rounding a bend at 1.6 miles, you can glimpse ahead the hunting club's main camp, which is located at the confluence of the West Branch and Long Pond Outlet.

Unfortunately, the easement requires paddlers to undertake a needless 0.3-mile carry to avoid passing in front of the main camp. Instead of a round-trip of seven miles with no portages, you get 6.4 miles of paddling

The West Branch on a blue-sky day. Photo by Phil Brown

and 0.6 miles of portaging. Nonetheless, this trip is the best option for those who want to experience the West Branch. Signs on the right indicate the start of the carry trail. Take out on the grassy bank and portage through a spruce forest to a put-in upstream of the camp.

Above the carry, the West Branch is narrower and often lined with alders. The views are not as good, but it's still an enjoyable paddle. You also may find the current stronger. In fact, you'll have to paddle hard in a few places to make progress.

It won't be obvious when you reach the third put-in. Look for a grassy island and a large solitary boulder. The put-in is to the right and just upstream of the boulder. A little farther upriver you can see rapids. If you make it this far, you will have traveled 3.5 miles, but given the strength of the current at the end, you may want to turn back a little earlier. Heading downriver, the return trip will be short and sweet.

DIRECTIONS: From Tupper Lake, drive west on NY 3 to Sevey Corners. Turn right onto NY 56 and drive 12.8 miles to Stark Road. Turn right and go 8.1 miles to Sterling Road. Turn right and 0.6 miles to a junction near a sign for the Five Mile Conservation Easement. Bear right and go 3.1 miles to a parking area on the right. To reach the put-in, continue a tenth of a mile down the road to a T-intersection, turn left, and park a little before the bridge over the river. Look for a carry trail on the right. After dropping off your boat, drive back to the parking area.

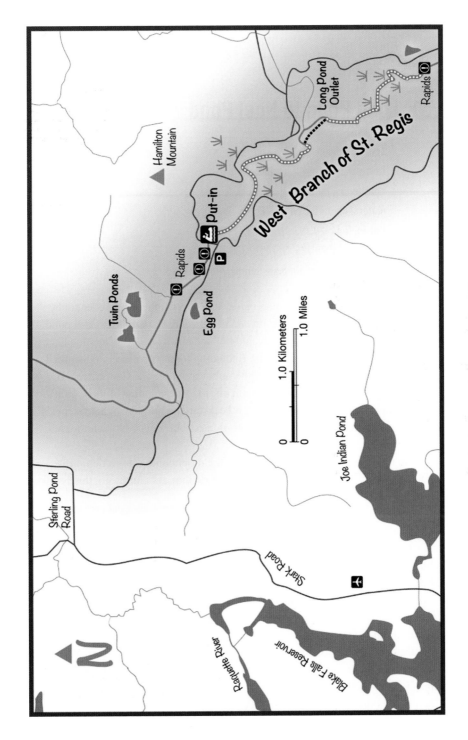

West Branch of St. Regis

Long Pond Outlet

Rapids

Hamilton Mountain

Put-in

Rapids

Twin Ponds

Egg Pond

P

1.0 Kilometers

1.0 Miles

Joe Indian Pond

Sterling Pond Road

Stark Road

Raquette River

Blake Falls Reservoir

N

51. Long Pond to Hoel Pond

Length: 7.5 miles
Carries: 3 totaling 0.5 miles
Shuttle: 5.4 miles
Motors: Permitted on Hoel Pond
Put-in: N 44°20.793', W 74°25.277'
Takeout: 44°20.785' N, 74°20.700'
National Geographic map: Saranac/Paul Smiths

For many people, pond-hopping in the St. Regis Canoe Area under sunny skies represents the *summum bonum* of Adirondack paddling. Each pond on the day's itinerary is a new adventure. Each has its own personality. Each is an invitation to experience nature (including loons) up close, undisturbed by motorboats. But paddling is not the only way to see the Canoe Area. A hike to the top of Long Pond Mountain affords a grand view of the region's glacial ponds, not to mention the High Peaks on the horizon. Whether this is the better perspective or not is a matter of taste, but you needn't choose one over the other.

On this trip, you visit five ponds and the mountaintop. It's a delightful paddle even if you forgo the hike, but don't do that. As climbs go, this is on the easy side: an elevation gain of 930 feet over 1.5 miles.

You'll need to drive or bicycle from Hoel Pond back to Long Pond. If you bike, fat tires are recommended as you'll be pedaling mostly on dirt roads. To avoid a shuttle, you could do a round-trip paddle from either pond to the Long Pond Mountain trail.

From the Long Pond parking lot, a wide trail leads a quarter-mile to a sandy put-in on the south shore. Looking across the pond, you can see Long Pond

Sheep laurel Photo by Phil Brown

Paddling up the outlet of Pink Pond. Photo by Phil Brown

Mountain about two miles away. To get to the start of the hiking trail, you paddle 2.3 miles in a horseshoe-shaped arc. First, though, you should pay a visit to Pink Pond. Paddle toward an island off the north shore about a half-mile away. Shortly before reaching it, look for the outlet of Pink Pond.

Sheep laurel, sundews, and pitcher plants are found along the stream's boggy shores. Pickerelweed and yellow and white water lilies grow in the channel. It's less than a quarter mile to the small pond. On its north shore, you can find a tiny stream that leads to Little Pink Pond. On the west shore is the outlet of Ledge Pond. In high water, you can paddle part way up this and then follow a path to Ledge Pond.

Upon returning to Long Pond, paddle east past the island. The pond soon bends north and passes through a narrow section. When you reach a bay with a view of the mountain, turn left and paddle through the bay to a shallow strait at its west end. Beyond the strait is another bay. Angle right toward the north shore: a small white sign marks the start of the hiking trail.

The marked trail leads to Mountain Pond in 0.6 miles, skirts the shoreline, and then begins the climb to the summit. From the open ledges, you can look

A good parking place at Slang Pond. Photo by Susan Bibeau

over the Canoe Area toward the High Peaks, including Mount Marcy and Algonquin Peak, the only two above five thousand feet. Hunt around and you'll find paths to other lookouts. The summit is a great place for lunch.

After returning to Long Pond, retrace your route through the two bays and then head east into another bay. Look for a white sign marking the start of a 0.2-mile carry to Slang Pond. Paddle southeast across this small water body to the outlet of Turtle Pond. If the water is low, you may have to walk your boat twenty yards up the shallow channel.

Turtle is substantially larger than Slang, with views of nearby peaks. Paddle to a culvert at the south end, where the outlet of Hoel Pond flows under railroad tracks. You might be tempted to pull your boat through the culvert, but it's probably easier to carry it over the tracks. Hoel Pond lies outside the Canoe Area. Consequently, you will see some houses on the east shore and perhaps some powerboats on the water. On the plus side, you will enjoy views of nearby peaks, including St. Regis Mountain, as you cross this large pond. The takeout is in Hoel's southeast corner; look for another white sign.

DIRECTIONS: From the village of Saranac Lake, drive north on NY 86 for a few miles to the blinking light at Donnelly's Corners. Turn left onto NY 186 and continue 9.4 miles to Floodwood Road (NY 186 turns into NY 30 after about 3 miles). Turn right and go 0.4 miles to Hoel Pond Road. Turn right and go 0.2 miles to a dirt lane on left (along a fairway on the Saranac Inn Golf Course). Follow the dirt lane about 0.3 miles to the shore of Hoel Pond. This is the takeout. To reach the put-in, return to Floodwood Road, turn right, and go 4.9 miles to a parking area on the right. The carry to Long Pond is 0.25 miles.

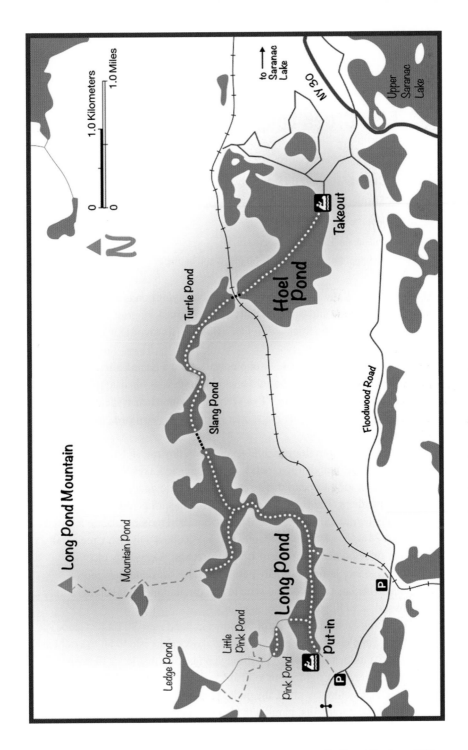

52. Fish Creek Loop

Length: 8.6 miles
Carries: 2 totaling 0.75 miles
Shuttle: No
Motors: Permitted/electric only
Put-in: 44°20.337' N, 74°24.316' W
National Geographic map: Saranac/Paul Smiths

Mark Bowie knows something about the beauty of ponds and streams: he took his canoe and camera all over the Adirondacks prior to publishing a book of photographs titled *Adirondack Waters*. His favorite waterway: Fish Creek.

"I've watched a bald eagle swoop upward from a bed of lilies, a large fish gripped in its talons, and alight on a pine to devour his catch," he has written about the quiet stream. "I've seen a great blue heron spear a catfish with his bill, deer feed in the bogs, otters frolic in the shallows, osprey wheel above."

On this trip—a rare loop paddle—you travel down Fish Creek for more than a mile and visit five ponds in the Saranac Lakes Wild Forest. In summer, when the two nearby state campgrounds are open, you're bound to see other paddlers. The route has far less traffic in spring and fall.

Paddlers will be happy to hear that gas-powered motorboats are allowed only on the two largest ponds, Floodwood and Rollins. On Fish Creek and the other three ponds, Copperas, Little Square, and Whey, only electric motors, up to five horsepower, are permitted. The *Adirondack Explorer* newsmagazine has called on the state to ban gas motors from Rollins and Floodwood as well, but so far to no avail.

You put in on the north side of Floodwood Pond near St. Regis Canoe Outfitters. Paddle south toward a large island. Keep the island on the right as you pass it and then turn left to go through a narrows that leads to the pond's east lobe. Follow the right shore to Fish Creek, the pond's outlet, reached at 1.3 miles. Just below the pond, the outlet passes under a bridge that connects two hiking trails that parallel the banks. Hemlock boughs hang over

A busy day on Fish Creek. Photo by Mark Bowie

the water. The current is barely perceptible; you might not notice it all if not for the bent water grass.

After 0.7 miles, the narrow stream reaches Little Square Pond. Unless you want to explore the pond, continue straight, following the left shoreline. Beyond Little Square, the stream widens considerably. A tamarack bog lies along the west shore. Nearly a half-mile from Little Square, Fish Creek starts to narrow again and turns to the left. Before reaching the turn, look for a channel hidden in the weeds to the right. It leads to Copperas Pond. Paddle across the conifer-ringed pond to a carry trail on the far end, marked by a white sign. Be sure to take the trail to Whey Pond, not the one to Black Pond. The carry is 0.65 miles.

Whey Pond, nearly three-quarters of a mile long, has a reputation as a good place to catch rainbow and brook trout. If you're an angler, you may have some competition: common loons fish here. In fact, they can be found on any of the ponds on this trip. Paddle to a sand beach on the far end of Whey and then carry less than a tenth of a mile to Rollins Pond.

You are now in the Rollins Pond State Campground. It and the neigh-

Lily pads in the shallows. Photo by Mark Bowie

boring Fish Creek Ponds State Campground have a total of 442 campsites. Rollins Pond is the quieter of the two: most powerboaters prefer to stay at Fish Creek Ponds, since it provides water access to Upper Saranac Lake. Rollins Pond is nearly two miles long. As you paddle north, look for Flood-wood Mountain to the northwest. A small island guards the entrance to the pond's north arm. After passing the island, follow the pond's right shoreline to the outlet. The short stream is shallow enough that you may have to walk your boat part of the way.

The stream leads you back to Floodwood Pond. You can see railroad tracks straight ahead. Turn right and pass through a narrows to the main body of the pond. Follow the left shore past a few houses and back to your starting point.

DIRECTIONS: From the village of Saranac Lake, drive north on NY 86 a few miles to the blinking light at Donnelly's Corners. Turn left onto NY 186 and go 9.7 miles to Floodwood Road (NY 186 turns into NY 30 en route). Turn right (west) onto Floodwood Road and go 4.2 miles to a parking area on the right near St. Regis Canoe Outfitters. The put-in at Floodwood Pond is on the other side of the road.

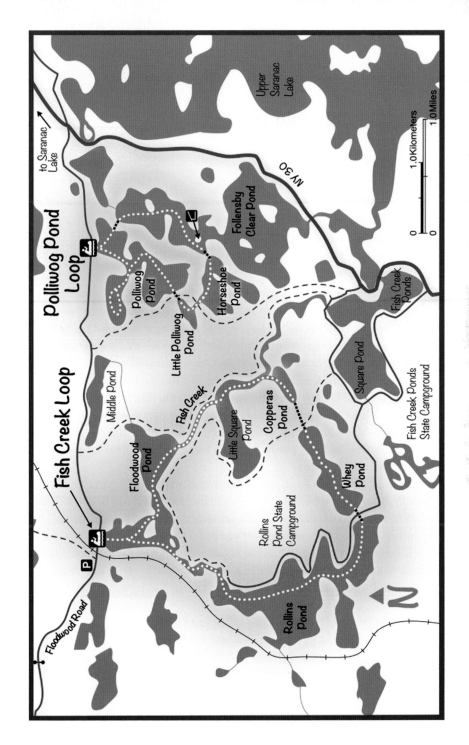

53. Polliwog Pond Loop

....

Length: 4 to 6 miles
Carries: 4 totaling 0.5 miles
Shuttle: None
Motors: Permitted
Put-in: 44°20.386' N, 74°21.048' W
National Geographic map: Saranac/Paul Smiths

The St. Regis Canoe Area lies to the north of Floodwood Road, but the glacial landscape of ponds and sinuous eskers that characterize the region can be found on both sides of the road. So similar is the topography that the land-use planner George Davis once recommended closing the road and expanding the Canoe Area south to encompass an additional twenty-six ponds.

As a matter of fact, a glance at a map reveals that the region south of Floodwood Road has a greater proportion of water to land than the Canoe Area and at least as many opportunities for pond-hopping. But where to begin? A good introduction is a circuit of Polliwog, Little Polliwog, Horseshoe, and Follensby Clear ponds. It entails four easy carries, the longest only two tenths of a mile.

Unlike in the Canoe Area, motorboats are allowed on these waterways. Usually, however, you won't see many and those you do see will be small. The motorboats have not kept loons, ducks, and other waterfowl from taking up residence. Indeed, you'd be unlucky if you didn't see several loons on this trip.

If you were to make a beeline for each carry trail, you could shorten the circuit to under four miles and finish it in a few hours, but there's no sense in hurrying. Stretch out the trip by exploring the ponds' bays, bogs, and islands.

Start at Polliwog Pond at a small beach just off Floodwood Road. After paddling south for 0.4 miles, turn right and follow a narrow channel into the pond's west arm. Loons sometimes visit this secluded bay. There is a boggy inlet on the north shore. The carry trail at the west end leads to Middle Pond (which is not part of this circuit). After returning to the main pond, round the peninsula on the right and then head southwest toward the short carry

The boggy end of Little Polliwog Pond. Photo by Phil Brown

trail (marked by a white sign) to Little Polliwog Pond.

A more apt name for this hidden jewel would be Very Little Polliwog Pond. If you paddle all out, you might make it to the next carry trail midway down the east shore in under a minute. A more worthwhile goal is to paddle to the bog at the south end of the pond and spend time among the water lilies, rose pogonia, bog laurel, and pitcher plants.

The next carry leads through a hemlock stand to the north bay of Horseshoe Pond. If you're not interested in exploring the bay, head for the end of the peninsula in the middle of the pond. The campsite on the peninsula's tip is a good place to stop for a picnic or swim.

The peninsula points in the direction of the carry trail to Follensby Clear, the largest of the four ponds. The short path leads to a put-in in the north basin, the less-busy part of the pond. Paddle north past an island lean-to, round a spit of land on the west shore, then head for a pair of islands, one small and one big (the latter has two campsites). After passing between the islands, angle left toward the trail that leads to Polliwog Pond. It's west of a trail that leads to Green Pond. Once back on Polliwog, you only need to cross the pond, angling north, to return to your starting point.

DIRECTIONS: From the village of Saranac Lake, drive north on NY 86 for a few miles to the blinking light at Donnelly's Corners. Turn left onto NY 186 and continue 9.4 miles to Floodwood Road (NY 186 turns into NY 30 after about 3 miles). Turn right and go 1.2 miles to Polliwog Pond on the left.

54. Seven Carries

Length: 6 miles
Carries: 6 totaling 0.9 miles
Shuttle: 7 miles
Motors: Permitted on Upper St. Regis Lake
Put-in: 44°23.716' N, 74°16.185' W
Takeout: 44°21.322' N, 74°17.532' W
National Geographic map: Saranac/Paul Smiths

Although the Adirondack Park offers many places to paddle, it has only one tract of Forest Preserve managed primarily for paddling: the St. Regis Canoe Area. The name promises much, and the place delivers: eighteen thousand acres of motor-free wilderness, fifty-eight ponds, twenty-four miles of hiking and carry trails, and seventy-five tent sites.

The state acquired most of the Canoe Area in 1898, and it has been wild ever since. Journeying from pond to pond, paddlers will see loons diving for fish, herons stalking minnows and frogs in the shallows, and stately white pines growing along the shores. Many of the ponds hold brook trout.

You could get lost in in the Canoe Area for a week, but for day-trippers, the best introduction may be the historical route known as the Seven Carries. In the 1800s, guides and visitors used it to travel between Paul Smith's hotel on Lower St. Regis Lake and the Prospect House on Upper Saranac Lake.

These days, many paddlers begin on Upper St. Regis Lake instead, but you could extend the trip by starting on Lower St. Regis (launching at Paul Smith's College). Also, most paddlers now end their trip short of Green Pond, the last pond on the original route. Thus, the modern route entails six carries, not seven.

Of course, you could do the through trip in either direction, but if you're doing a round-trip to St. Regis Pond—a good option if a shuttle cannot be arranged—you should start in the north, whether at Lower or Upper St. Regis Lake. One advantage of the round-trip is that you avoid the longest carry (a half-mile). You'll miss out on one pond, Little Clear, but in compensation you'll get to see the others twice.

The tiny channel leading to Bog Pond. Photo by Phil Brown

From the public landing on Upper St. Regis, you can see St. Regis Mountain and its fire tower in the west. The mountain will stay with you for most of the trip. Upon putting in, head in the general direction of the peak, keeping parallel to the south shore. The large wetland on the left is Roiley Bog. After passing a pair of islands, start scanning the shoreline ahead for a white sign that marks the start of the carry to Bog Pond.

Reached at 0.7 miles, the wide trail leads 150 feet to a DEC register. Put in the tiny channel nearby. It winds a short distance through a wet tangle of leatherleaf, Labrador tea, and bog rosemary that may account for the pond's name. The pond itself is only a few hundred feet long, which is its charm.

At the far end of Bog, pick up the short trail to Bear Pond. Once on the water, paddle around a peninsula, turning left and passing two small islands to reach the next carry trail. During the 0.4-mile trip across Bear Pond, you enter the St. Regis Canoe Area. The peninsula and its lean-to, however, are private property.

In the nineteenth century, travelers carried from Bear to a small pond known as Turtle or Middle and thence to Little Long Pond, according to Edwin R. Wallace's guidebook from that era. Today's carry trail goes straight to Little Long, ascending a low ridge to arrive at the shore in 0.15 miles. Perhaps most travelers bypassed the little pond even in Wallace's day; otherwise, the route would have been dubbed the Eight Carries.

On Little Long, paddle south to a narrows that connects the pond's two lobes. When the pond opens again, bear right. Heading up the lake, you have good views of St. Regis Mountain. Angle toward the left shore to find the next carry, which begins near a big white pine. The trip across Little Long is 0.85 miles.

An easy 0.15-mile portage brings you to the north shore of Green Pond, which Wallace praised as "one of the clearest gems that spangle the wilderness." Do not make the mistake of paddling to the white sign on the opposite shore. That is the start of a carry to Little Clear Pond. Rather, paddle to the right toward the west shore. In just a quarter-mile, you arrive at the takeout for perhaps the shortest carry of the day, about a hundred feet to St. Regis Pond. All told, you've now paddled and portaged 2.9 miles.

At 380 acres, St. Regis Pond is one of the largest lakes in the Adirondacks entirely surrounded by Forest Preserve. It's also one of the prettiest, with its wild shoreline, wooded islands, and views of peaks near and far. The pond is the source of the West Branch of the St. Regis River. The best way to see the whole pond is to paddle one and a half miles to its western tip, where the river begins its journey to the St. Lawrence. If you're doing a round-trip and paddle the length of St. Regis Pond, your excursion will be about nine miles. Alternative turnaround points are the lean-to about two-thirds of the way down the lake or one of the islands.

If your goal is to take the direct route to the Little Clear Pond carry, round the big point at the south end of St. Regis Pond and follow its shoreline to a black spruce/tamarack bog. A channel leads through the bog to a boardwalk.

Having paddled and portaged 4.1 miles, you now face the last and longest carry of the day: a half-mile to the northwest corner of Little Clear. Not far from the start of the path, bear left at a trail junction (the way right leads to the Fish Pond Truck Trail). From the sandy put-in, you can see a large wetland to the right that beckons exploration. To reach your final destination, however, you need to head southeast toward the pond's narrow waist. En route you may spot signs on the east shore for carry trails to Green Pond and Grass Pond.

Advancing down the pond, you enjoy views of the western High Peaks. After passing a few islands, aim for the takeout at a parking area in the pond's southwest corner. DEC breeds salmon in Little Clear for stocking elsewhere, so fishing is prohibited unless you're a loon.

DIRECTIONS: From the village of Saranac Lake, drive a few miles north on NY 86 to the blinking light at Donnelly's Corners. Turn left onto NY 186 and go 4.0 miles to Lake Clear Junction, where NY 186 meets NY 30. From here you either continue straight to go to the takeout at Little Clear Pond or turn right (north) to go to the put-in at Upper St. Regis Lake. For the takeout: continue straight 2.8 miles to Fish Hatchery Road. Turn right and go 0.5 miles to a dirt road. Turn right and go 0.2 miles to a large parking area on the right, just past the railroad tracks. For the put-in: from Lake Clear Junction, drive north on NY 30 for 3 miles to St. Regis Carry Road. Turn left and go 0.3 miles to the public landing.

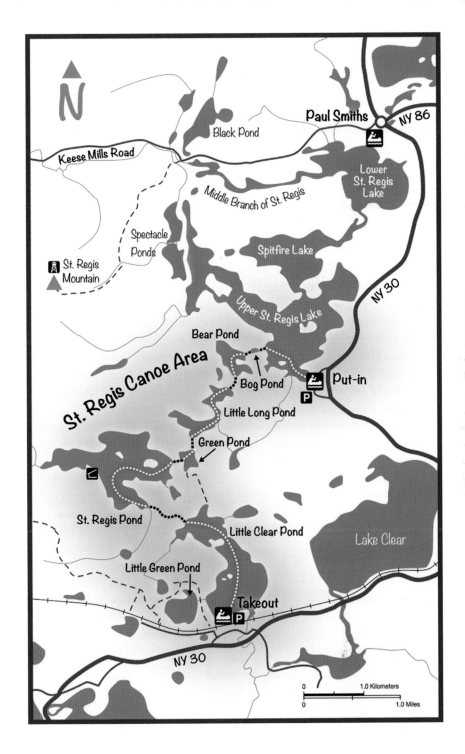

N

Paul Smiths

NY 86

Black Pond

Keese Mills Road

Lower St. Regis Lake

Middle Branch of St. Regis

Spitfire Lake

Spectacle Ponds

St. Regis Mountain

NY 30

Upper St. Regis Lake

Bear Pond

St. Regis Canoe Area

Bog Pond

Put-in

Little Long Pond

Green Pond

St. Regis Pond

Little Clear Pond

Lake Clear

Little Green Pond

Takeout

NY 30

0   1.0 Kilometers

0   1.0 Miles

55. Sixteen-Mile Level on Middle Branch of St. Regis

Length: 12 miles round-trip
Carries: 0.7 miles
Shuttle: No
Motors: Permitted
WSR status: Scenic
Put-in: 44°29.972' N, 74°25.553' W
National Geographic Map: Saranac/Paul Smiths

Nineteenth-century writers extolled Sixteen-Mile Level on the Middle Branch of the St. Regis both as a sportsman's paradise, teeming with trout and deer, and as a place of great beauty. After an 1883 visit, the Adirondack surveyor Verplanck Colvin described the level as "a picturesque stillwater which winds for miles through rich alluvial lands, now among alders and bushy swamps, and now through natural meadows."

Colvin's description remains apt today. Back then, though, Colvin fretted over plans to flood the region to facilitate lumbering. "It is to be regretted that the State is not the owner of this beautiful valley," he wrote in a report to the legislature.

More than a century later, in 1998, the state partially fulfilled Colvin's wish by purchasing about half the level from Champion International. Access is still not easy: from Blue Mountain Road, a seasonal dirt thorough-fare, paddlers must carry or wheel their boats 0.7 miles to the put-in. On the plus side, the portage adds to the river's sense of remoteness and increases your chances of finding solitude. It also keeps motorboats away.

When it bought the land, the state expected that pad-dlers would be able to take

Common muskrat Photo by Larry Master

Azure Mountain as seen from the Middle Branch of the St. Regis. Photo by Phil Brown

out farther downriver, shortly before a one-lane bridge on Blue Mountain Road. Later, officials discovered that the proposed takeout and parking area were on private land. Theoretically, you could exit the river before the private land and thrash your way to the road, but the lack of a proper takeout is only part of the problem. The final portion of an end-to-end trip would require five carries, totaling 1.3 miles (in addition to the carry to the initial put-in), with precious little paddling in between. What's more, some of the carries are veritable bushwhacks.

Until these problems are resolved, the best option for flatwater paddlers is a twelve-mile round trip. Of course, this necessitates portaging to and from the put-in. Fortunately, the carry trail follows an old woods road that's easy to walk.

From the put-in, a sandy beach near large pines, the river is navigable in both directions, but if you go upstream you soon reach private land. The downstream float, in contrast, lies entirely within the Forest Preserve.

At the start, the east side of the river is forested. Within a mile, you leave the woods behind as the Middle Branch wends its way north through Meno Bog, characterized by mossy peatland, sedge meadows, and alder thickets. It's great habitat for ducks, herons, and other birds. You might also see signs of otter and muskrat.

Throughout most of the trip, you enjoy views of the surrounding peaks.

Enjoying lunch on the river. Photo by Phil Brown

The most conspicuous are Buck Mountain in the south and Azure Mountain in the north. After your paddle, you might want to hike up Azure from Blue Mountain Road. The trail is only a mile, and the views from the summit cliffs and fire tower are superb.

After nearly six miles, you come to the first rapids. These are easy enough that you might be tempted to run them or line your boat, but they are soon followed by larger rapids. In all, there are four sets of rapids en route to the proposed takeout. So most flatwater paddlers will want to turn around here.

On the return trip, look for the hidden mouth of Quebec Brook, which enters from the east a few miles upstream from the rapids. You can meander for more than a mile up the brook. Paddlers have gone all the way to Blue Mountain Road via the brook, but it entails a good amount of thrashing. It's easier to return to the road the way you came in.

DIRECTIONS: From NY 30 in Paul Smiths, turn west onto Keese Mill Road, just north of the entrance to Paul Smith's College. At 7.4 miles, a mile after a sharp right bend, the road crosses the Middle Branch on a steel-deck bridge. From here continue five miles to the put-in parking area on the left. The road crosses the river again in another 4.5 miles, just past the proposed takeout.

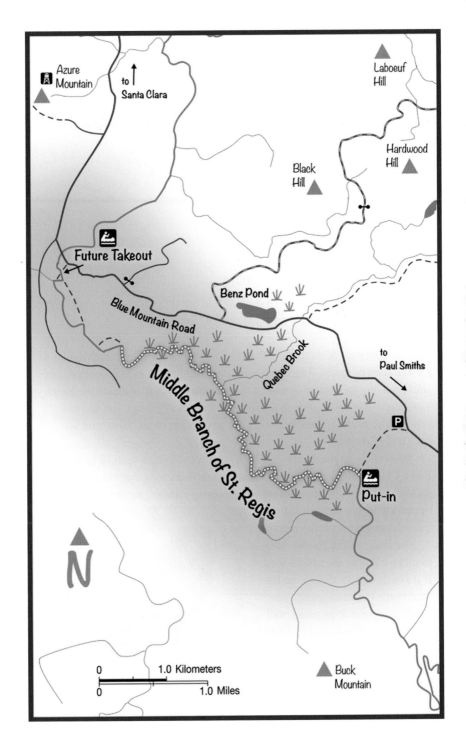

Azure Mountain

to Santa Clara

Laboeuf Hill

Hardwood Hill

Black Hill

Future Takeout

Blue Mountain Road

Benz Pond

Quebec Brook

to Paul Smiths

P

Middle Branch of St. Regis

Put-in

N

0   1.0 Kilometers
0   1.0 Miles

Buck Mountain

56. Middle St. Regis to Santa Clara Flow

Length: 8 miles

Carries: 2 totaling 0.6 miles

Shuttle: 8 miles

Motors: Permitted

WSR status: Recreational

Meander quotient: 35%

Put-in: 44°33.332' N, 74°27.930' W

Takeout: 44°37.837' N, 74°27.200' W

National Geographic map: Saranac/Paul Smiths

Most Adirondack rivers flow from the wild to civilization. The Middle Branch of the St. Regis embodies this paradigm in miniature. Paddlers start on a tiny backwater channel and finish on a wide flow above the Santa Clara dam. But civilization is relative: the hamlet of Santa Clara has few year-round residents, and you won't see any homes on the river until the very end of the trip.

You can avoid the shuttle and both carries by doing a round-trip from Santa Clara Flow. Starting from the state boat launch on the flow, you can paddle six miles upstream before encountering rapids. The downside of the round-trip is that you miss out on the wildest stretch of the river.

For those opting for the end-to-end trip, there are two caveats. If it's early spring, make sure the road to the put-in is open. After winter, the road stays gated until maintenance crews rake it. And if you plan on a bicycle shuttle, be aware that you'll be pedaling for miles on dirt roads. Fat tires are recommended.

From the parking area for

Red-winged blackbird Photo by Larry Master

Santa Clara Flow near the takeout. Photo by Phil Brown

the put-in, you have a 0.15-mile portage to the river: after carrying around a vehicle barrier, continue down the road a few hundred feet and look for a path on the right. It ends at a grassy bank along a backwater channel. To reach the main river, go downstream a short distance and pull your boat over a low grassy bank. (For a pleasant diversion, you can paddle upstream on the backwater channel for a half-mile or so.)

Continuing downstream, you pass a campsite on the left about a half-mile from the put-in. The river winds through marsh and swampland. Besides the ubiquitous alder, other shrubs growing along the banks include wild raisin, mountain holly, and dogwood. If you look back at the right time, you will see Azure Mountain to the southwest. A mile-long trail leads from Blue Mountain Road to the summit. The views from Azure's cliffs and fire tower are outstanding.

At 1.25 miles from the put-in, you come to a giant boulder in the stream, about fifteen feet high. The current quickens and the smooth surface gives way to riffles. At 1.5 miles, you reach the rapids. Look for a boulder near the right shore with an arrow pointing to the carry trail. It begins near a campsite and leads in 0.4 miles to an alder swamp along the river. Although the trail ends here, the rapids do not. You have to paddle or line your boat through the last few hundred feet of shallow whitewater or drag it along the shore to a safe put-in.

Below the rapids, nothing but calm water lies ahead. As you progress,

The quiet backwater above the put-in. Photo by Phil Brown

the channel widens and so do the views—of Azure and other peaks. You're likely to see a variety of waterfowl, including mallards, common mergansers, and Canada geese, in the grassy shallows. Red-winged blackbirds often call from the marshy shores. You also pass a number of beaver lodges, but there are no dams to obstruct your passage.

If you happen to notice a no-trespassing sign along the shore, feel free to ignore it: the state purchased the river corridor from Champion International in the late 1999—with the exception of an old railroad bed. The river passes under the rail bed's bridge a few miles below the rapids. The bed is now owned by a hunting club. Stay off it: there are plenty of other places to stop to have a snack or take in the scenery.

About a mile from the bridge, the river broadens considerably. In another 0.75 miles, it makes a sharp right turn and passes an attractive campsite on the left, situated among white pines on a rocky bluff. Turning another corner, the river widens again, affording views to the north of cliffs on The Pinnacle (another easy hiking destination). The main part of the flow can get choppy in a breeze. When you see a camp on the west shore and start to hear cars on Route 458, you have less than a half-mile to go reach the dock at the boat launch and return to civilization.

DIRECTIONS: From NY 458 in Santa Clara, turn south on Dexter Road, which starts just west of the bridge over the Middle Branch. Drive 0.1 miles and turn left into the parking lot for the state boat launch on Santa Clara Flow. This is the takeout. To reach the put-in, return to Dexter Road, turn left, and go 0.3 miles to a T-intersection. Bear left and go 2.7 miles to Blue Mountain Road. Turn left and go 3.9 miles to a dirt road on the left marked by a DEC sign. If the gate is open, drive down this road 0.4 miles to a fork. Bear left and go another 0.6 miles to a parking area.

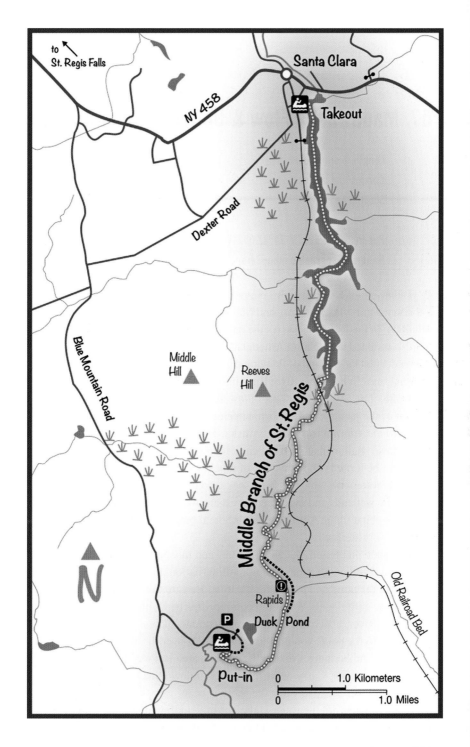

57. Madawaska Flow & Upper Quebec Brook

Length: 8 miles round-trip
Carries: 0.4 miles
Shuttle: No
Motors: Prohibited
Put-in: 44°31.321' N, 74°22.552' W
National Geographic map: Saranac/Paul Smiths

Madawaska is a surprisingly common toponym. You can find it on maps of New Brunswick, Ontario, and Maine as the name of rivers and communities. In the Adirondacks, it's the name of a pond. Interpretations of the word—assumed to be Native American in origin—are commonplace too. The contenders include "Land of Porcupines," "People of the Shallows," "Never Frozen," and "Where One River Runs into Another with Water Grass."

None of these fits Madawaska Flow as well as Edwin R. Wallace's variant of the name found in his nineteenth-century travelogue *Descriptive Guide to the Adirondacks:* Muddywaska. The pond is not only mucky, but it's often so shallow that paddlers can't help stirring up the bottom.

Don't be turned off by this talk of muck. Madawaska happens to be a gorgeous waterway, with grassy tussocks, floating bog mats, and piney islands. The wetlands and evergreen forest around the pond constitute some of the best habitat in the Adirondacks for boreal birds. The pond itself harbors a variety of waterfowl.

The state purchased Madawaska Flow and most of Quebec Brook, the pond's inlet and outlet, from Champion International in 1999. On this trip, you put in the pond and paddle up the inlet. Be sure to save some time to explore the entire pond. You could combine this trip with an excursion up the Onion River, which is described in a separate chapter.

To get to the pond, you must drive six miles over dirt roads through commercial timberlands. Next to the parking area is a woods road blocked by a vehicle barrier. Carry or wheel your boat down this road for 0.4 miles, then turn left off the road when the shore is near.

Tufts of grass dot the water at the put-in. Paddling due south toward more open water, you soon reach the mouth of Quebec Brook. The inlet is

Madawaska Flow with Rice Mountain in the background. Photo by Phil Brown

broad, with almost no current. As on the flow, the glassy surface is decorated with water lilies and other aquatic plants. Heading upstream, look for Rice Mountain to make an appearance on the left. Farther on you'll be able to see Jenkins and St. Regis mountains in the south. A few miles from the pond, you come to an island with the remains a hunting camp. On the east shore of the brook is a camp that's still in use on private land. In a half-mile, you pass a smaller island with a rusting vehicle.

The farther you go, the narrower the boggy stream gets. Eventually, you reach private land, but the boundary is not marked. If you come to an obvious fork, you have crossed into private property and should turn around.

When you return to the flow, paddle across to the west end to explore the large floating bogs. Olive-sided and alder flycatchers often hang out in the wetlands on this end of the pond. Other boreal birds that dwell in the vicinity of Madawaska include the gray jay, black-backed woodpecker, and boreal chickadee. The spruce grouse, now endangered in New York State, once lived in these parts as well but is thought to be extirpated.

Quebec Brook continues as the outlet on the other side of a dam at the north end of the pond. The dam enlarged the original waterway and thus accounts for the second part of the pond's name: a flow is a water body formed by flooding land. Like others of its ilk, Madawaska is a charm to paddle.

DIRECTIONS: From the intersection of NY 30 and NY 86 in Paul Smiths, drive north on NY 30 for 9 miles to NY 458. Turn left and go 1.4 miles to Madawaska Road, marked by a DEC sign on the left. Drive 6 miles to the parking area, bearing left at 0.4 and 1.1 miles and right at 5 miles. To reach the put-in, walk down the gated road.

Note: Shortly before this book went to press, a landowner closed the road leading to the parking area. DEC was working to restore access. If the road remains closed, paddlers can get to Madawaska by paddling and portaging up Quebec Brook from Blue Mountain Road.

The Onion River in fall. Photo by Phil Brown

58. Onion River & Lower Quebec Brook

Length: 9.6 miles round-trip
Carries: 2 totaling 0.7 miles
Shuttle: None
Motors: Prohibited
Put-in: 44°31.321' N, 74°22.552' W
National Geographic map: Saranac/Paul Smiths

They say the Onion is the only river in the Adirondacks that flows into a brook, which is your first clue that it's not the mightiest of streams. It is, however, one of the most charming. You can go up the Onion only a mile and half, but to get to the river you paddle two other delightful waterways, Madawaska Flow and Quebec Brook. In all, you can get in nearly ten miles of paddling—more if you combine this excursion with a trip up the flow's inlet.

The Madawaska tract—a longtime destination of birders—was purchased by the state from Champion International in 1999 and now belongs to the Forest Preserve. However, a hunting club still owns the old railroad bed that crosses Quebec Brook a little north of the flow. Getting to the Madawaska parking area requires a six-mile drive along dirt roads through commercial timberlands. Near the trail register is a gated road leading west. To reach the most convenient put-in on the flow, carry along the road for 0.4 miles until you see the water close by on the left. Leave the road to put in on the flow.

Your first objective is to paddle a mile across the flow to the outlet dam. At the put-in, the flow is very shallow, dotted with grassy tussocks. After launching, head toward a wooded island to the southwest. You need to go left around the island. If you try going right, you'll become mired in the marsh. Once past the island, look for open water on the right (to the north). This will lead you to the outlet, Quebec Brook.

Take out left of the dam and put in on the brook on the other side of an old woods road. This is a continuation of the road you walked in on. You could portage all the way from the parking area to the dam, but unless you have a wheeled cart, you'd have to lug your boat for a mile, and besides you'd miss out on paddling the flow.

Upon entering Quebec Brook, you pass through a small cattail marsh where you might flush a heron. After the cattails, the brook is bordered by grasses and shrubs. You can see Jennings Mountain dead ahead and Rice Mountain to your right. On the left is the embankment of the railroad bed. At 0.4 miles, you reach the Onion's mouth on the right. The river is quite broad at the start, with hardly any current. Like the brook, it's bordered by shrubby peatland that affords wide views. Conifers grow in the lowlands, while hardwoods dominate the hillsides. In fall, the green conifers and multicolored hills provide a pleasing contrast.

Expect a few beaver dams. You may be able to paddle over them, but be prepared to get out and pull your boat across one or two if the water is low. A mile upriver, the Onion braids in a marsh. Bear left to stay in the main channel. Soon after, the stream narrows considerably as alder thickets close in. At 1.2 miles, progress is stopped by a large beaver dam. Most people probably will not want to continue, but if you carry over the dam, you can push on for another quarter-mile or so before you run out of water and elbow room.

Once you've seen all the Onion has to offer, return to Quebec Brook. You now have the option of heading back to your car (for a six-mile round-trip) or exploring more of Quebec Brook (for a ten-mile round-trip). If you opt for the latter, turn right and head downstream. Presently, you come to the charred ruins of a low railroad bridge. If you lie flat you may be able to squeeze under, but it's safer to carry around.

Numerous tamaracks—the only conifers that shed their needles annually—grow in the wetlands that borders both sides of the brook. Although the state now owns Quebec Brook, you occasionally see old no-trespassing signs by the shore.

You pass over a few low beaver dams before reaching boulders and rapids, a mile and a half below the Onion. When the brook is high enough, whitewater enthusiasts can run the Quebec down to Blue Mountain Road. If you're flatwater paddler, however, you'll want to turn around at the head of the rapids. On your return trip, you may want to paddle among the bog islands on the west end of Madawaska Flow.

DIRECTIONS: From the intersection of NY 30 and NY 86 in Paul Smiths, drive north on NY 30 for 9 miles to NY 458. Turn left and go 1.4 miles to Madawaska Road, marked by a DEC sign on the left. Drive 6 miles to the parking area, bearing left at 0.4 and 1.1 miles and right at 5 miles. To reach the put-in, walk down the gated road.

Note: Shortly before this book went to press, a landowner closed the road leading to the parking area. DEC was working to restore access. If the road remains closed, paddlers can get to Madawaska by paddling and portaging up Quebec Brook from Blue Mountain Road.

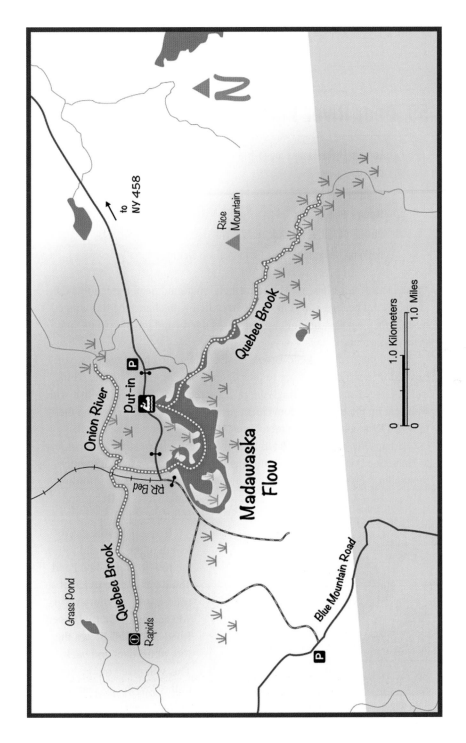

N

Grass Pond

Quebec Brook

Rapids

Onion River

Put-in

P

to
NY 458

Rice
▲ Mountain

Quebec Brook

RR Bed

Madawaska
Flow

Blue Mountain Road

P

0   1.0 Kilometers
0   1.0 Miles

59. Deer River Flow

Length: Up to 9 miles round-trip
Carries: None
Shuttle: No
Motors: Permitted
Put-in: 44°37.991' N, 74°16.778' W
National Geographic map: Saranac/Paul Smiths

The Deer River Flow may be an artificial impoundment, but it abounds in natural beauty. You'll find marshes filled with chattering red-winged blackbirds, bogs that harbor carnivorous sundews and pitcher plants, and numerous scenic vistas.

If you put in along Cold Brook Road at the south end of the flow, you can paddle nearly three miles to the concrete dam on the north end. Built in 1904, the dam is surprisingly large: a few hundred feet long, with a wide walkway on the top. It's a convenient picnic spot that offers views up the flow of Debar and Baldface mountains, two of the area's highest peaks.

Perhaps the best part of the flow is the east fork, a riverine arm that leads to Horsehoe Pond. You enter it midway down the flow. At first, it's quite broad, but it eventually narrows into a winding, marshy stream, affording more views of Debar and Baldface.

Bald eagle Photo by Larry Master

If you travel the entire length of the flow and follow the fork to Horseshoe Pond, you'll get in nine miles of paddling. For a shorter trip, you can put in on Red Tavern Road and paddle down the fork to the dam and back. This will give you the best of the flow in less than five miles.

On Deer River Flow's east arm, looking toward Debar Mountain. Photo by Phil Brown

The put-in on Cold Brook Road is a small strip of sandy shoreline. A sign warns users to check their boats for Eurasian milfoil, an exotic aquatic weed that has taken root in the flow. The flow's shallow waters are quite hospitable to milfoil. Fortunately, they also discourage the use of large motorboats, which would churn up the weed and spread it around. Typically, the occasional motorboat seen on the flow is a small outboard owned by an angler fishing for bass, pike, or perch.

From the launch site, follow a channel through the lily pads and cattails to the broader part of the flow. There is a residence on the western shore. Otherwise, this part of the flow is undeveloped, with forest on the west side and wetlands on the east. Expect to see great blue herons, geese, or other

Serenity on Deer River Flow. Photo by Ray Palmer

waterfowl. Bald eagles also have been sighted.

Paddling down the flow, look for Furnace Mountain on the left. After 1.5 miles, you reach the east fork on the right. Continuing on, you pass the privately owned Deer River Campsite on the right and then a large home on the left. Soon after this, you pass two small islands before arriving at the dam at 2.8 miles. If you want to stop, take out on the left. Downstream of the dam, the Deer River is frothy whitewater, and the land is posted.

After visiting the dam, return to the east fork. Like the rest of the flow, the fork is shallow, with old stumps sticking up here and there. For the best scenery, paddle up the fork at least a mile to the bridge on Red Tavern Road. From here, there is a marvelous view across the marsh toward Debar and Baldface. Horseshoe Pond is about a half-mile beyond the bridge. This small pond has several camps and offers views of the small peaks in the neighborhood, including Humbug Mountain.

DIRECTIONS: From the junction of NY 30 and NY 86 in Paul Smiths, drive north on NY 30 for 15.4 miles to Cold Brook Road on the left. Just after making the turn, you'll see the put-in on the right. Note that there are two entrances to Cold Brook Road. You want the second, or northernmost, one. Red Tavern Road is a few miles north of Cold Brook Road. To reach this put-in, turn west off NY 30 and drive about a half-mile to a small bridge.

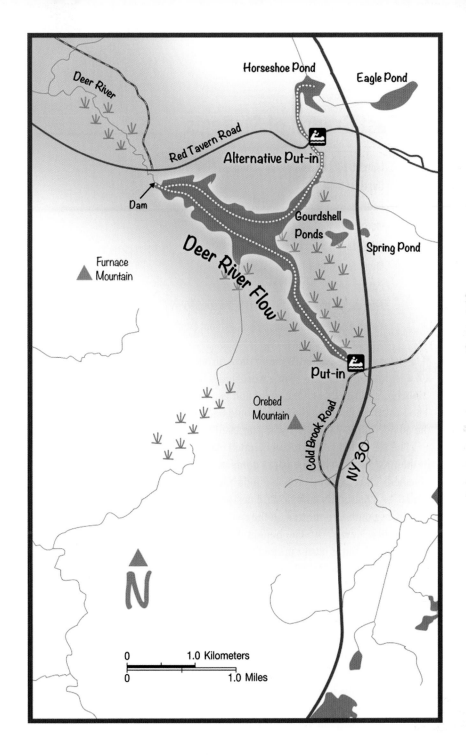

Deer River

Horseshoe Pond

Eagle Pond

Red Tavern Road

Alternative Put-in

Dam

Gourdshell
Ponds

Spring Pond

Deer River Flow

Furnace
Mountain

Put-in

Orebed
Mountain

Cold Brook Road

NY 30

N

0   1.0 Kilometers

0   1.0 Miles

60. East Branch of St. Regis

Length: Up to 20 miles round-trip
Carries: None
Shuttle: No
Motors: Permitted
WSR status: Scenic
Meander quotient: 42%
Put-in: 44°40.283' N, 74°25.544' W
Alternative put-in: 44°38.234' N, 74°24.030' W
National Geographic map: Saranac/Paul Smiths

Most rivers designated Wild by the Adirondack Park Agency are too remote or too frothy—in a word, too wild—to appeal to flatwater canoeists and kayakers. One exception is the Oswegatchie below High Falls. The East Branch of the St. Regis would be another if the state had followed the advice of the naturalists who surveyed the river in the 1970s.

The APA's field crew recommended classifying as Wild eight miles of the East Branch, but the paper company that then owned the corridor objected. The company probably didn't want to upset the hunters and fishermen who leased its land: a Wild designation would have prevented them from using outboard motors on the river.

In 1999, New York State bought the eight-mile stretch from Champion International, but it hasn't upgraded the classification. Since the river sees very little motorboat traffic, such a change might be seen as largely symbolic. Nevertheless, paddlers can take pleasure in knowing that this part of the East Branch meets the criteria of Wild rivers: it is free of development and inaccessible except by water or trails.

From Everton Falls, where the river drops twenty feet, you can paddle ten miles upstream before encountering lengthy rapids (and private land). This heavenly stretch of flatwater is known as the Nine-Mile Level, a moniker that sells it a little short. The Adirondack Chapter of the Nature Conservancy owns the put-in, located on the little-traveled Red Tavern Road, as well as about a mile and a half of river above the falls. The rest of

Spotted Joe-Pye weed adorning the banks of the East Branch.   Photo by Phil Brown

the way you'll be in the public Forest Preserve.

The river winds through a valley that once held a postglacial lake. The marshy cul-de-sacs, grassy meadows, and alder thickets attract a variety of birds, such as great blue herons, cedar waxwings, red-winged blackbirds, common mergansers, belted kingfishers, and olive-sided flycatchers. You also can expect to see a number of beaver lodges and perhaps a few of the denizens. Fortunately, though, you will encounter few beaver dams, if any, that impede progress.

At 1.3 miles from the put-in, just beyond a huge boulder on the left shore, the channel divides around an island. Bear right, for the left channel is usually impassable. As you go around the island, you have to paddle hard in two spots—the only quick water on the entire trip.

For much of the route you enjoy views over wild meadows of low hills that border the river valley. In season, you can see many kinds of wild-flowers mingled with the grasses or growing along the water's edge. In other stretches alders occupy the riverbank. Occasionally, the river pulls close to the conifer forest that stands on the edge of the floodplain.

Paddling past brown alders in early spring. Photo by Susan Bibeau

At 4.9 miles, you pass an alternative put-in on the right. As of 2011, it was marked only by a red ribbon, so it may be hard to spot. Paddlers can use this put-in to get to the upper reaches of Nine-Mile Level more quickly. The parking area is down a dirt road off State Route 458. There is a five-minute carry to the river.

Just beyond the put-in is an unusually long straightaway, but the East Branch thereafter resumes its winding ways. At 5.8 miles you pass a campsite on the left, marked by a yellow disk barely visible through the vegetation. The site is above a tall sandbank at a right bend in the river.

At 9.9 miles, the current strengthens when you come to a bouldery section. Just beyond is a privately owned footbridge and a long rapid, so the boulders are a good place to reverse course. The turnaround is five miles above the alternative put-in. If you started at the Red Tavern Road put-in, on the return trip you should be able to shave an hour or two off the time it took to paddle upstream. But any time is well spent on a wild river—even if it isn't Wild.

DIRECTIONS: From the junction of NY 30 and NY 86 in Paul Smiths, drive north on NY 30 for 17.5 miles and turn left on Red Tavern Road (County 14). Go 8.1 miles to a parking lot on the right. The put-in is across the road.

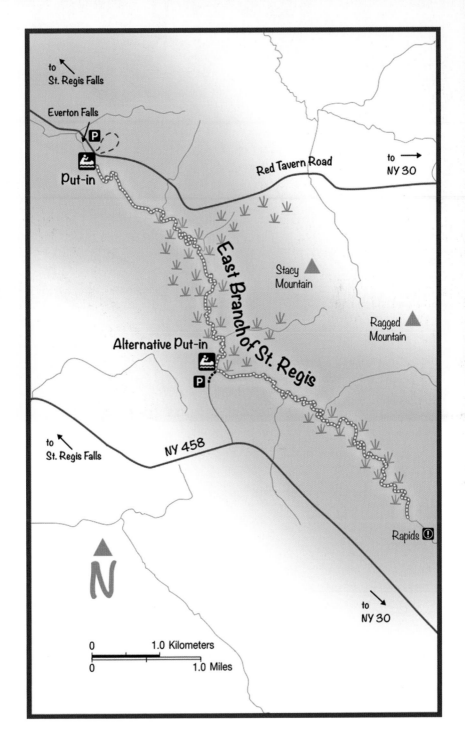

to St. Regis Falls

Everton Falls

P

Put-in

Red Tavern Road

to NY 30

East Branch of St. Regis

Stacy Mountain

Ragged Mountain

Alternative Put-in

P

to St. Regis Falls

NY 458

Rapids ①

N

0   1.0 Kilometers

0   1.0 Miles

to NY 30

Photo by Larry Master

Appendices

....

Multiday trips

Northern Forest Canoe Trail

The Northern Forest Canoe Trail stretches 740 miles from the Adirondacks to northern Maine. The New York State section is 147 miles, starting in Old Forge and ending on Lake Champlain. The first 130 miles lie within the Adirondack Park.

The Adirondack segment includes all or portions of seven trips in this book: **Browns Tract Inlet** (page 148), **Forked Lake & Brandreth Lake Outlet** (page 141), **Axton to Raquette Falls** (page 32), **Stony Creek Ponds & Raquette River** (page 35), **Middle & Lower Saranac Lakes** (page 39), **Round the Mountain** (page 44), and **Saranac River** (page 48).

The Northern Forest Canoe Trail folks have published thirteen full-color maps for the entire route. The first three maps cover the New York section: Fulton Chain of Lakes to Long Lake, Long Lake to Saranac River, and Saranac River to Lake Champlain. The maps include information about natural and human history and describe milestones along the waterways.

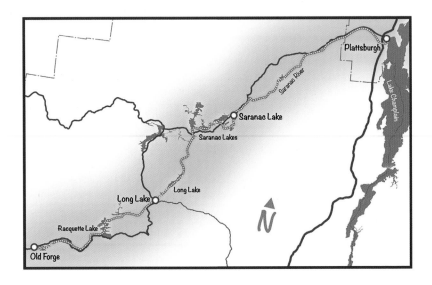

The confluence of the Saranac River and Moose Creek. Photo by Jill Wenner

National Geographic's maps cover only the Adirondack segment, spread over four sheets: Old Forge/Oswegatchie, Northville/Raquette Lake, Lake Placid/High Peaks, and Saranac/Paul Smiths. The Adirondack Paddler's Map covers the route from Long Lake to Union Falls Pond.

Paddling the New York portion of the NFCT could take up to three weeks. You might also want to pick up *The Northern Forest Canoe Trail: The Official Guidebook.* Published by the NFCT organization, the book offers detailed descriptions of the waterways and portages. It's designed to be used in conjunction with the NFCT maps.

THE ROUTE: From Old Forge, paddle and portage up the Fulton Chain to the end of Eighth Lake, carry to Browns Tract Inlet, paddle downstream to Raquette Lake and down the lake to its northeastern tip, carry to Forked Lake, paddle to Forked's east end, paddle and portage the Raquette River to Long Lake, paddle down the lake to the Raquette River and downriver to Raquette Falls, carry around the falls and continue downriver to Stony Creek, paddle up the creek and through Stony Creek Ponds, carry to Upper Saranac Lake, paddle to end of southeast bay, carry to Middle Saranac Lake, paddle across Middle Saranac and down Saranac River to Lower Saranac Lake, paddle to First Pond, Second Pond and Saranac River, follow river to Oseetah Lake, paddle down Oseetah to Lake Flower, take out in village of Saranac Lake, and return to Saranac River to portage and paddle the river the remaining sixty-three miles to Lake Champlain.

Whitney Loop

This wild, scenic loop links four of the routes in this book: **Little Tupper Lake to Rock Pond** (page 194), **Lake Lila** (page 190), **Bog River to Hitchins Pond** (page 200), and **Round Lake** (page 198). The forty-five-mile circuit includes more than twenty carries and takes about a week to complete. Many paddlers choose to end the trip at the lower dam on the Bog River, a variation known as the Whitney C. It's also possible to do only portions of the loop, starting at Little Tupper and ending at Lake Lila (the Lila Traverse) or starting at Lila and ending at the lower dam.

National Geographic's Old Forge/Oswegatchie map shows all the waterways in the loop, but not all the carries. A better choice for this trip is the Adirondack Paddler's Map, which includes all the carries.

THE ROUTE: Paddle from Little Tupper Lake to Rock Pond, carry to Hardigan Pond, paddle to the end of Hardigan, carry to Salmon Lake Outlet, paddle downstream to Little Salmon Lake, carry to Lilypad Pond, paddle across Lilypad and carry to Shingle Shanty Brook,* paddle downstream to Lake Lila and across Lila to Harrington Brook,

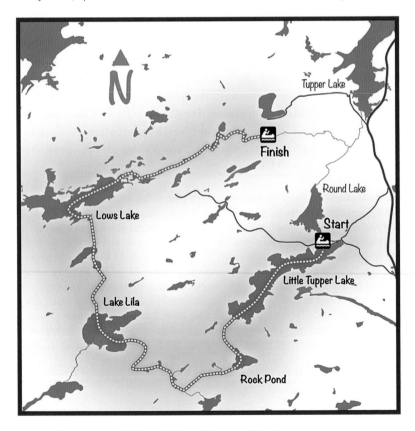

Crossing Lake Lila. Photo by Susan Bibeau

portage and paddle upstream to Rainer Brook and up the brook to railroad tracks, carry along tracks to carry trail on left, carry to Clear Pond, paddle to north shore of Clear, carry to Bog Lake, paddle to Lows Lake and down lake to upper dam, carry to Hitchins Pond, and paddle across pond and down Bog River to takeout at lower dam. To finish the loop, paddle and portage down the Bog River to Round Lake Outlet, carry up the outlet to Round Lake, and paddle from Round back to Little Tupper. Unless you're a whitewater expert, you will be portaging far more than paddling on this part of the loop.

*It would be possible to avoid this carry by paddling from Lilypad Pond to Mud Pond, carrying around short rapids, and following Mud Pond's outlet to Shingle Shanty. However, this necessitates paddling and portaging through private land. The author did this route in 2009 and was sued by the landowners. The state contends the route should be open to the public under the common-law right of navigation. As this book went to press, the dispute was still unresolved.

Oswegatchie Traverse

This spectacular route passes through some of the wildest country in the Adirondack Park. The beginning and end of the trip are covered in the chapters on **Bog River to Hitchins Pond** (page 200) and **Oswegatche River to High Falls** (page 186).

Allow at least three days for the thirty-five-mile journey, more if you

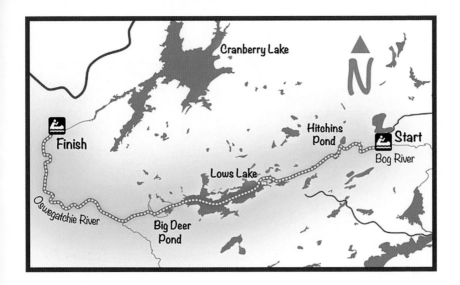

want to linger in the wild or take side trips. Possible excursions include climbing Grass Pond Mountain and hiking through old-growth forest to the Five Ponds.

The route has two short and two long carries. The big ones are from Lows Lake to Big Deer Pond (0.8 miles) and from the pond to the Oswegatchie (2.2 miles).

The trip ends at a grassy clearing known as Inlet, once the site of a hotel. From here it's a fifty-five-mile shuttle back to the starting point at Lows Lower Dam.

It's possible to travel in a loop and avoid a shuttle, though doing so will add twenty-six miles and a few days to the trip. Below Inlet, the Oswegatchie flows through a series rapids, but you can follow a trail that parallels the river about two miles to Wanakena, where you can put back in and paddle to Cranberry Lake. After crossing the lake, you can follow another trail about four miles to Grass Pond, whence you paddle to Lows Lake and return to the lower dam.

You can use either National Geographic's Old Forge/Oswegatchie map or the Adirondack Paddler's Map.

THE ROUTE: From the lower dam, paddle up Bog River to Hitchins Pond, cross Hitchins and carry to the upper dam, paddle up Lows Lake to its western end, carry to Big Deer Pond, paddle across pond and carry to Oswegatchie River, paddle downriver to High Falls, carry around falls and continue downriver to takeout at Inlet. To complete the loop, carry to Wanakena, put back in river and paddle to Cranberry Lake, cross lake to Chair Rock Flow, carry to Grass Pond, paddle to Lows Lake, and return to lower dam.

Nine Carries Plus

The 15-minute map that covers the St. Regis Canoe Area boasts more than 150 lakes and ponds. "To canoeists," Paul Jamieson wrote, "this generous display of blue nudity is the centerfold of Adirondack topographical maps." This book describes two day-trips in the Canoe Area, but many paddlers will want to spend more time in this magnificent region.

The Nine Carries is a traditional route that can be paddled and portaged in a long day, but it's better savored over two or three days. The Nine Carries has a few variations. The one suggested here is described by Jamieson in *Adirondack Canoe Waters: North Flow.* If you follow the route in a clockwise direction (Jamieson describes it in reverse), you have a choice upon reaching St. Regis Pond. To complete the traditional route, carry to Little Clear Pond. A more adventurous option is to follow the Seven Carries route to Upper St. Regis Lake. This will up the number of water bodies visited (and carries) to thirteen. Other ponds can be reached by short side trips

Long Pond in the St. Regis Canoe Area. Photo by Mark Bowie

along the Nine Carries, including Bessie Pond, Lydia Pond, and Mud Pond.

The traditional Nine Carries route is about twelve miles, including about five miles of portaging. The Nine Carries Plus route is a little longer, with roughly the same amount of portaging. Both incorporate parts of the book's two day trips: **Seven Carries** (page 230) and **Long Pond to Hoel Pond** (page 220). Both National Geographic's Saranac/Paul Smiths map and the Adirondack Paddler's Map show the entire Canoe Area.

THE ROUTE: Carry to Long Pond and paddle to its north bay, carry to Nellie Pond, paddle across Nellie and carry to Kit Fox Pond, paddle across Kit Fox and carry to Little Long Pond (there are two in the Canoe Area), paddle to Little Long's north shore and carry over esker to Little Fish Pond, paddle to Little Fish's northeast corner and carry to Fish Pond, paddle to Fish's east end and carry to Ochre Pond, paddle across Ochre and carry to St. Regis Pond, paddle to St. Regis's south tip and carry to Little Clear Pond, and paddle down Little Clear to the takeout. For the longer trip, follow the Seven Carries route when you get to St. Regis Pond, portaging to and paddling, in succession, Green Pond, the other Little Long Pond, Bear Pond, Bog Pond, and Upper St. Regis Lake. You can finish at Upper St. Regis or continue to Paul Smith's College on Lower St. Regis Lake.

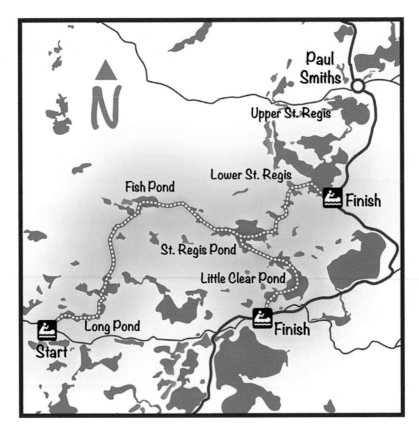

Rainbow Lake. Photo by Susan Bibeau

Arc of the Rainbow

The nice thing about this route is that you can paddle for several days and still end up, in the village of Saranac Lake, with a fairly short shuttle of seventeen miles—short enough to bicycle.

The route described here is about forty-five miles, but you could extend it by visiting more ponds in the St. Regis Canoe Area and adding in several of the ponds in the Fish Creek region.

Most of the route is described in the following chapters: **Rainbow Lake & North Branch of the Saranac** (page 68) ; **Jones Pond, Osgood Pond & Osgood River** (page 60); **Seven Carries** (page 230); **Middle & Lower Saranac Lakes** (page 39); and **Round the Mountain** (page 44).

The Adirondack Paddler's Map shows the entire route. If you use the National Geographic maps, you will need Saranac/Paul Smiths and Lake Placid/High Peaks.

THE ROUTE: Start at the northeast end of Lake Kushaqua and paddle to the west end of Rainbow Lake, via Clear Pond and Inlet. Carry to Jones Pond, paddle across pond and down outlet to Osgood Pond, paddle around point on Osgood's south shore to reach hand-dug canal, follow canal to Little Church Pond, follow another canal to Church Pond. Carry to Paul Smith's College on Lower St. Regis Lake, paddle through Spitfire Lake to Upper St. Regis Lake and then follow route of Seven Carries to takeout at Little Clear Pond. Carry to Little Green Pond, paddle across Little Green to southwest shore, follow trails to NY 30, and put in at boat launch at Saranac Inn. Paddle down Upper Saranac Lake to eastern end of Saginaw Bay, carry to Weller Pond, paddle to Middle Saranac and then Saranac River, follow river to Lower Saranac Lake, paddle down lake to First Pond, continue to Second Pond and Saranac River again. Follow river to Oseetah Lake, paddle down Oseetah to Lake Flower, and take out in village of Saranac Lake.

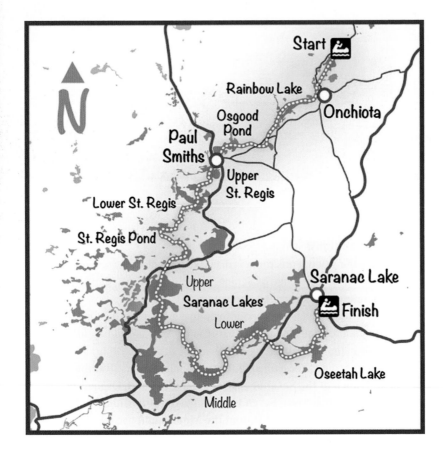

A summer day on Browns Tract Inlet. Photo by Phil Brown

Old Forge to Oz

This route traces a large arc through the western Adirondacks, linking parts of three of the long-distance routes already described: the Northern Forest Canoe Route, the Whitney Loop, and the Oswegatchie Traverse. It's roughly 130 miles, including numerous carries, so allow ten days or more for the journey. The shuttle is about a hundred miles.

Pieces of the route are described in detail in the chapters on **Browns Tract Inlet** (page 148), **Forked Lake and Brandreth Lake Outlet** (page 141), **Axton to Raquette Falls** (page 32), **Lake Lila** (page 190), and **Oswegatchie River to High Falls** (page 186).

Most of the route is shown on National Geographic's Old Forge/Oswegatchie map, but you'll also need Nat Geo's Northville/Raquette Lake

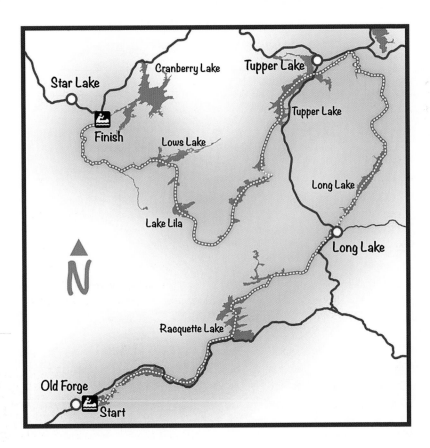

and Lake Placid/High Peaks maps. The two Adirondack Paddler's Maps also cover the route. The Adirondack Council's Bob Marshall Wild Lands Complex map shows all of the route except for a piece of Long Lake and a stretch of the Raquette River.

THE ROUTE: Starting in Old Forge, follow the route of the Northern Forest Canoe Trail as far as Stony Creek. Continue down the Raquette River to Tupper Lake, cross Tupper to the mouth of the Bog River, carry around Bog River Falls and paddle upriver to Round Lake Outlet, carry to Round Lake and paddle to Little Tupper. Follow the route of the Whitney Loop to Lows Lake. Once on Lows, head west and follow the route of the Oswegatchie Traverse.

Meander quotients

While researching this book, I canoed numerous streams that wind through alder swamps, marshes, and fields of tussocks. I like the intimacy of small streams: the grass swaying in the breeze, the splashes of wildflower, the insistent call of the red-winged blackbird, the animal tracks in the mud—everything is right there. And you never know what's around the next bend.

But they are twisty! I started to wonder what was the twistiest of them all. To find out, I came up with a statistic I call the meander quotient.

First, I use a GPS watch to measure the actual distance paddled. When I get home, I fetch the appropriate National Geographic map and measure the straight-line distances at one-inch intervals along the river's depicted course. I add these up and subtract the total from the actual distance. This yields the overall distance I deviated from the straight and narrow—meandering, if you will. I divide the result by the actual distance to arrive at a ratio, which I then convert to a percentage.

A bird's-eye view of South Inlet. Photo by Phil Brown

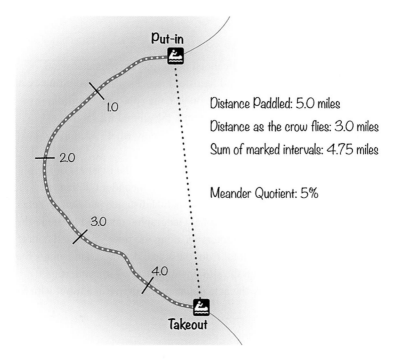

Put-in

1.0

2.0

3.0

4.0

Takeout

Distance Paddled: 5.0 miles
Distance as the crow flies: 3.0 miles
Sum of marked intervals: 4.75 miles

Meander Quotient: 5%

To give an example: I paddled the Schroon River above Schroon Lake for 8.1 miles, yet the sum of my straight-line distances was only 4.0 miles. So we calculate as follows:

- **8.1 – 4.0 = 4.1**
- **4.1 ÷ 8.1 = 0.51 = 51%**

As it turns out, the Schroon is one of the twistiest rivers in the book.

You may wonder why I measure straight-line distances at intervals along the river rather than simply measure the direct distance from the put-in to the takeout. I did it this way to avoid distortions created by big bends. In the illustration, the river does not meander, but it has one turn of ninety degrees. The actual distance paddled from A to B is 5.0 miles. The direct distance between the two points is 3.0 miles. This would yield a meander quotient of 40%, which suggests the river is a lot twistier than it actually is. The interval method yields a distance of 4.75 miles and a meander quotient of 5%.

The quotient's accuracy likely is proportional to the length of river measured. Whatever its flaws, the meander quotient allows reasonable comparisons of the twistiness of Adirondack rivers. The table on the following page lists the meander quotients of thirty-two waterways. The quotients represent an average. Sections of these rivers are twistier than indicated.

Waterway	Miles Paddled	Meander Quotient	Comments
Jordan	5	52%	
Upper Schroon	8.1	51%	
Miami	2.8	50%	
Jessup	4.1	48%	
North Moose	11.5	48%	
Grass River	4.9	46%	Lampson Falls trip
Alder Bed Flow	4.3	45%	
Oswegatchie	9.4	45%	
Grass River	6.6	44%	Massawepie Mire
East St. Regis	10.2	42%	
West Oswegatchie	1.75	41%	Upstream trip
Lower Oswegatchie	7.5	38%	
West Sacandaga	7.9	38%	
West St. Regis	3.5	38%	Includes carry
Brandreth Lake Outlet	3	37%	
Kunjamuk	3.6	37%	
Lower Osgood	7.5	37%	
Middle Moose	5.9	37%	
Raquette	12.9	37%	Falls to Crusher
Browns Tract Inlet	2.75	35%	
Middle St. Regis	8	35%	Santa Clara trip
Bog	2.25	34%	To Hitchins Pond
Chubb	3.3	33%	
Fall Stream	4.8	33%	To Vly Lake
West Ausable	5.3	31%	
Boreas	2.2	30%	
Dunham Marsh	2.1	29%	
Little	4	28%	
Saranac	8.5	27%	To Moose Pond Rd.
Marion	3.9	19%	
Lower Hudson	13.4	14%	
Upper Hudson	4.1	5%	To Opalescent

Wildflowers on the waterways

Wildflowers add greatly to the enjoyment of paddling. Following are some of the flowers that frequently grow in the water and along the shores in the Adirondacks. The months indicate when they are in bloom.

Fragrant water lily (*Nymphaea odorata*). Beautiful white lily with yellow center. Grows in still waters up to five feet deep. Flowers often close by midafternoon on sunny days. June to September.
Photo by Phil Brown

Yellow pond lily (*Nuphar variegata*). Globe-shaped flower that sticks out of the water like a yellow periscope. Common in shallow, quiet waters of ponds, lakes, and rivers. Notched broad leaves float on the surface. Also called spatterdock. May to September. Photo by Phil Brown

Pickerelweed (*Pontederia cordata*). Spikes of violet-blue flowers often found in shallow, placid waters. Large heart-shaped leaves. Seeds and leaf stalks have been used as food. July to August.
Photo by Phil Brown

Turtlehead (*Chelone gabra*). Two-lipped flowers resemble the heads of turtles. Found in low wet areas and along streams. July to September.
Photo by Phil Brown

ABOVE: Spotted Joe-Pye-weed (*Eupatorium maculatum*). Plants grow up to six feet tall, with fuzzy pinkish flowers clustered on top of purplish or purple-spotted stalks. Common along streams and in wet places. Whorls of lance-like leaves. July to September.
Photo by Phil Brown

Cardinal flower (*Lobelia cardinalis*). Scarlet flowers on tall stalks along streams and in other wet places. Pollinated by ruby-throated hummingbirds. July to September.
Photo by Phil Brown

Swamp candles (*Lysimachia terrestris*). Yellow flowers form dense clusters along the stalk. Five tapering petals, arranged like the points of a star. Found in swamps, bogs, and marshes and along shores. June to August. Photo by Phil Brown

Northern pitcher plant (*Sarracenia purpurea*). Purple-veined leaves collect water that drowns insects so plant can absorb nutrients from its prey. Purplish flower on leafless stalk. Common in bogs. Photo by Nancie Battaglia

Roundleaf Sundew (*Drosera rotundifolia*). Carnivorous bog plant with white or pinkish flowers at end of slender stalks. Sticky droplets at tips of leaves' tentacles snare insects. June to September. Photo by Mike Lynch

Rose pogonia (*Pogonia ophioglossoides*). Pink orchid of bogs, swamps, and wet meadows. A single lance-shaped leave is found midway up the slender stem. June to August. Photo by Phil Brown

Blue flag (*Iris versicolor*). Showy purplish flower abundant in marshes, bogs, and swamps and along shores. Tall swordlike leaves (the name *flag* comes from Middle English *flagge*, meaning reed). May to August. Photo by Phil Brown

Purple-fringed orchid (Platanthera psycodes). Lavender flowers grow in clusters that form a spike on the upper stem. Found along streams, swamps, and other wet places. June to August.
Photo by Larry Master

Leatherleaf (*Chamaedaphne calyculata*). Evergreen shrub with thick, waxy leaves and white bell-shaped flowers. Abundant in bogs and along wet shores. Blooms in spring. Photo by Jerry Jenkins

Labrador tea (*Ledum groenlandicu*). Low evergreen shrub with clusters of white flowers (five petals) growing at the end of hairy stalks. Early settlers made tea with the leaves. Found in bogs. June to August. Photo by Jerry Jenkins

Buttonbush (*Cephalanthus occidentalis*). Shrub whose small tubular flowers form white balls, accounting for the common name. Grows in swamps and along streams and ponds. June to August.
Photo by Phil Brown

List of bird photos

Larry Master, a zoologist and accomplished photographer, contributed the pictures of birds that appear throughout the book. They are species often seen or heard by paddlers. The page numbers of the photos are listed below.

American bittern (*Botaurus lentiginosus*), **177**
Bald eagle (*Haliaeetus leucocephalus*), **248**
Black-backed woodpecker (*Picoides arcticus*), **202**
Belted kingfisher (*Ceryle alcyon*), **50**   Photo by Jeff Nadler
Boreal chickadee (*Poecile atriapillus*), **153**
Chestnut-sided warbler (*Setophaga pensylvanica*), **94**
Common loon (*Gavia immer*), **162**
Common merganser (*Mergus merganser*), **164**
Gray jay (*Persisoreus canadensis*), **66**
Great blue heron (*Ardea herodias*), **216**
Lincoln's sparrow (*Melospiza lincolnii*), **54**
Mallard (*Anas platyrhynchos*), **180**
Palm warbler (*Setophaga palmarum*), **62**
Pied-billed grebe (*Podilymbus podiceps*), **132**
Red-winged blackbird (*Agelaius phoeniceus*), **238**
Spotted sandpiper (*Actitis macularius*), **81**

You can find more samples of Master's photography at **masterimages.org.**

Those who want to learn more about Adirondack birds should consult *Adirondack Birding: 60 Great Places to Find Birds*, by John M.C. Peterson and Gary N. Lee (published by ADK and Lost Pond Press). Many of the waterways in *Adirondack Paddling* are also birding hotspots.

Map resources

All of the waterways in this book can be found on National Geographic's Trails Illustrated maps of the Adirondack Park. These full-color sheets are great for finding roads, put-ins, hiking trails, lean-tos, and other facilities. The hiking trails are numbered and color-coded to refer to the corresponding trail descriptions in the Adirondack Mountain Club's guidebooks. The maps distinguish between the public Forest Preserve and private property.

The maps can be purchased separately on the club's website for $11.95 each or as a set for $49.95. They also are sold in outdoor-gear stores. National Geographic numbers the maps as follows:

#742 Lake Placid/High Peaks
#743 Lake George/Great Sacandaga
#744 Northville/Raquette Lake
#745 Old Forge/Oswegatchie
#746 Saranac/Paul Smiths

The Saranac/Paul Smiths map encompasses the St. Regis Canoe Area and adjacent ponds, much of the Adirondack Park's lake belt, and many of the north-flowing rivers. It covers in full nineteen of the trips in this book, nearly a third of the total, and a portion of a twentieth. The Old Forge/Os-wegatchie map covers fifteen trips; Lake Placid/High Peaks, eleven (plus part of another); Northville/Ra-quette Lake, ten; and Lake George/Sacandaga, four.

These other maps may be of interest to canoeists and kayakers:

Adirondack Paddler's Map. Published by St. Regis Canoe Outfitters, this large color sheet covers the Saranac Lakes, St. Regis Canoe Area, the William C. Whitney Wilderness Area, and many northern rivers. It sells for $19.95 on the St. Regis Canoe Outfitters website. It also is sold in stores. The fifth edition corrects a number of mistakes. St. Regis publishes a separate map for the southwest part of the Park, including the Fulton Chain of Lakes, Raquette Lake, and Blue Mountain Lake. It sells for $9.95.

Northern Forest Canoe Trail.
Mountaineers Books has published a thirteen-map series that covers the entire 740-mile Northern Forest Canoe Trail (see page 258). The first three maps cover the New York leg, from Old Forge to Lake Champlain. The full-color, water-resistant maps can be bought on the Northern Forest Canoe Trail website for $9.95 each.

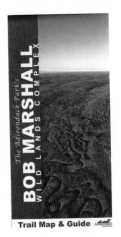

Trail Map & Guide

Bob Marshall Wildlands Complex. The Adirondack Council has published a large, full-color map of the western Adirondacks that covers many waterways described in this book. The map shows hiking trails and canoe routes, among other things. It not only differentiates between Forest Preserve and private land, but it also indicates which of the private lands are protected by conservation easements. The map can be obtained for free on the council's website. It also is available at tourist-information centers.

Raquette River Outfitters. This Tupper Lake canoe outfitter has published a color, water-resistant map of the Bog Lake-Lows Lake region. The mapmaker relied on satellite imagery to create an accurate representation of shorelines. It's smaller than the Adirondack Paddler's Map, but just as detailed and easier to use. The map includes hiking trails and campsites. It sells for $12.50. Raquette River Outfitters plans to make similar maps of other paddling destinations.

USGS topos. Paddlers who want more topographical detail can obtain U.S. Geological Survey maps. Paper copies can be purchased on the survey's website or in gear stores. Digital copies can be downloaded for free from the website.

Adirondack Park Explorer 3D. National Geographic sells a software program ($29.95) that includes all of its Trails Illustrated maps for the Park. The software allows you to print out color

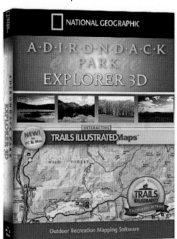

maps, plot routes and waypoints, create elevation profiles, find GPS coordinates, and search for toponyms. It is one of several mapping programs on the market.

Adirondack ADK Mountain Club

The Adirondack Mountain Club (ADK) is dedicated to the protection and responsible recreational use of the New York State Forest Preserve, and other parks, wild lands, and waters vital to our members and chapters. The Club, founded in 1922, is a member-directed organization committed to public service and stewardship. ADK employs a balanced approach to outdoor recreation, advocacy, environmental education, and natural resource conservation.

ADK encourages the involvement of all people in its mission and activities; its goal is to be a community that is comfortable, inviting, and accessible.

The Adirondack Mountain Club is a charitable organization, 501(c)(3). Contributions are tax deductible to the extent the law allows.

30,000 members count on us, and so can you:

- We produce the most-trusted, comprehensive trail maps and books
- Our outdoor activities take you all around the world
- Our advocacy team concentrates on issues that affect the wild lands and waters important to our members and chapters throughout the state
- Our professional and volunteer crews construct and maintain trails
- Our wilderness lodges and information centers give you shelter and direction

Benefits of Membership include:

- Fun outdoor recreation opportunities for all levels
- *Adirondac* magazine (bimonthly)
- Special rates for ADK education and skill-building programs, lodging, parking, publications, and logo merchandise
- Rewarding volunteer opportunities
- Supporting ADK's mission and thereby ensuring protection of the wild lands and waters of New York State

Lodges and campground

Adirondak Loj, on the shores of Heart Lake, near Lake Placid, offers year-round accommodations in private and family rooms, a coed loft, and cabins. It is accessible by car, and parking is available.

The Adirondak Loj Wilderness Campground, located on ADK's Heart Lake property, offers thirty-two campsites and sixteen Adirondack lean-tos.

Johns Brook Lodge (JBL), located near Keene Valley, is a backcountry facility accessible only on foot and open on a seasonal basis. Facilities include coed bunkrooms or small family rooms. Cabins near JBL are available year-round.

Mount Jo's view of Heart Lake and the High Peaks. Photo by Carl Heilman II

Both lodges offer home-cooked meals and trail lunches. Member discounts are available at all lodges and the campground.

Visit us!

ADK centers in Lake George and on our Heart Lake property near Lake Placid offer ADK publications and other merchandise for sale, as well as backcountry and general Adirondack information, educational displays, outdoor equipment, and snacks.

Contact Us:

ADK Member Services Center (Exit 21 off I-87, the Northway)
814 Goggins Road Lake George, NY 12845-4117
www.adk.org   Information: 518-668-4447
Membership, donations, publications, and merchandise: 800-395-8080

ADK Heart Lake Program Center (at Adirondak Loj on Heart Lake)
PO Box 867
1002 Adirondack Loj Road
Lake Placid, NY 12946-0867
Educational programs and facility reservations: 518-523-3441

ADK Public Affairs Office
301 Hamilton Street
Albany, NY 12210-1738
Public Affairs: 518-449-3870

PHIL BROWN is the editor of *Adirondack Explorer*, a newsmagazine that focuses on environmental issues and outdoor recreation in the 5.8-million-acre Adirondack Park. In 2006 he founded Lost Pond Press to publish *Bob Marshall in the Adirondacks*, an anthology of the writings of a pioneering conservationist and legendary hiker. Lost Pond has also published *Adirondack Birding*, a guidebook by John M.C. Peterson and Gary N. Lee, and *Within a Forest Dark*, an award-winning novel by Michael Virtanen. When he isn't mucking about with words, Phil is usually out hiking, paddling, rock climbing, or cross-country skiing.

The *Adirondack Explorer* is a nonprofit publication that focuses on environmental issues, outdoor recreation, and the culture of the Adirondack Park. For more information, visit **AdirondackExplorer.org**.

INDEX

....

Many of the waterways also are mentioned in the appendix on multiday trips.